DELICIOUS
LAUGHTER

DELICIOUS LAUGHTER

Rambunctious Teaching Stories
from the *Mathnawi*
of
Jelaluddin
Rumi

versions by Coleman Barks

MAYPOP

Cover: "Night on Vega Beach," by Herb Creecy. Other Creecy
paintings may be seen by contacting the artist himself: Herb Creecy,
27 Market St. Barnesville, GA 30204 (404) 358-1687

RUMI: Delicious Laughter

$7.50/copy, plus $1.00 postage and handling.
25¢ postage for each additional book.
Order from:
MAYPOP BOOKS
196 Westview Drive
Athens, GA 30606
(404) 543-2148

ISBN: 0-9618916-1-0
Library of Congress Catalog Card Number: 89–092396

for
Andrew Dick

CONTENTS

These titles are not Rumi's. They are whims of my own. Rumi is content with a one-word title for the entire six volumes: *Mathnawi*, which means, simply, "Couplets." It places the work in a Near Eastern tradition of wisdom compendiums, though Rumi's, certainly, breaks all the traditional moulds. Adding titles here may be a misleading convenience. These are not discrete (or discreet) poems, in any sense. They are buckets lifted from a whole, whose connectedness runs its vast and intricate course, well apart from any naming.

SCRIMSHAW

Some of these poems contain the "Latin Parts" of Reynold Nicholson's edition of Rumi's *Mathnawi*.† Nicholson translated the entire six books of the *Mathnawi* into English, but he cast some sections into Latin, presumably, to hide things he thought were unseemly. Until now, these stories involving sexual predicaments, and such winsomely-taboo subjects as flatulence and defecation, have remained hidden under their Latinate coverings.

Certain of these poems however, may even today shock, and perhaps offend, some readers. The 13th Century *was* an age of kings and concubines, and the imagery of sexism and of the seeming glorification of war are not acceptable terms any longer for whatever wisdom we might have. But we should remember that these stories are not primarily about people. The characters here represent *impulses* within people, which can act and change, for the better or the worse. Rumi's world is a tangle of creatures, all in their guided and misguided ways, participating in a Cosmic Play, which can be called the gradual Union of the personal with God, or soul-growth, or evolving consciousness. The terms don't matter to Rumi. The *experience* they point to, though, is his constant joy and the deep poetic energy that rises within him.

Everything is a metaphor for this poet. Muhammed said the *Greater* war (Jihad) is the struggle inside the Self. For Rumi, anything that human beings do, any cruelty, any blindness, resonates with wisdom about the inner life. Any love-impulse especially, however distorted, moves as part of a larger Wanting. Moments of sexual shame, erections and their sudden droopings, a clitoral urgency that admits no limit, the mean impulse to play a sexual trick on one's mate—these are recognizable behaviors, and Rumi does not so much judge them as hold them up for a lens to look into the growth of the soul, which is the deep subject behind these stories.

All the action takes place within a larger question, and an even wider Laughter. There are several comedic modes here: The Bosch-like grotesquerie of the Gourdcrafting poem (p. 135), the Chaucerian slapstick of the Captain's bare-assed running around (p.43), the secret tenderness of Nasuh's change (p. 3). But they all involve a breaking-open. Nasuh's comes at the moment of possible sexual embarrassment. It happens to the Caliph when the beautiful woman laughs at his impotence (p. 46). It happens to the immoderate guest when he sees the Prophet washing the soiled bedclothes. (p. 79). It happens in the moments of greatest vulnerability.

These teaching stories are a kind of scrimshaw—intricately carved, busy figures, in confused and threatening and weirdly funny situations—curving on the slope and stillness of a colossal tooth. The characters are guilty, lecherous, mean, gluttonous, tricky, and finally, opened. Rumi relishes the scribbled energy of each story, even as he asks, "What is this giant tooth hungry for?" There are no easy answers for that. These heroes, and heroines, move toward a bursting open point, about which Rumi is ambivalent.

He seems to want to leave the reader in the jaws of a predicament, pulled, for example between the two fierce and plausible arguments of "A Man and a Woman Arguing," which ends without ending, "This argument continued throughout the day, and even longer."

Rumi has many strategies for mirroring the complexities of soul growth: A wildly extravagant comedy, a severe toughness about the discipline necessary, an ecstatic sweetness that comes in the visionary moments, etc. Shams himself said of Rumi, "Each day I observe in him some state, or quality which was not there before.... He speaks fine words, but don't be satisfied with them. Behind each is something you should ask him."

This collection is full of that rich elusiveness, so like light-changes on a body of water.

Coleman Barks
December 8, 1989

† Nicholson, R.A., The Mathnawi of Jalaluddin Rumi, 8 vols., London: Luzac & Co., 1925-40. Critical edition, translation, and commentary.

Nasuh

Some time ago there was a man named Nasuh.
He made his living shampooing women in a bathhouse.
He had a face like a woman, but he was not effeminate,
though he disguised his virility, so as to keep his job.

He loved touching the women as he washed their hair.
He stayed sexually alert, at full strength,
all the time, massaging the beautiful women,
especially the Princess and her ladies-in-waiting.

Sometimes he thought of changing jobs,
of doing something
where he wouldn't be so constantly lustful,
but he couldn't quit.

He went to a gnostic saint and said,
"Please remember me in a prayer."

That holy man was spiritually free,
and totally opened to God. He knew Nasuh's secret,
but with God's gentleness he didn't speak it.

A gnostic says little, but inside he is full of mysteries,
and crowded with voices. Whoever is served
that Cup keeps quiet.

The holy man laughed softly and prayed aloud,
"May God cause you to change your life
in the way you know you should."

The prayer of such a Sheikh is different
from other prayers. He has so completely dissolved

his ego, nothing-ed himself, that what he says
is like God talking to God. How could
such a prayer not be granted?

The means were found to change Nasuh.
While he was pouring water into a basin
for a naked woman, she felt and discovered
that a pearl was missing from her earring.

Quickly, they locked the doors.
They searched the cushions, the towels, the rugs,
and the discarded clothes. Nothing.
                          Now they search
ears and mouths and every cleft and orifice.

Everyone is made to strip,
and the Queen's lady chamberlain
probes one by one
the naked women.
                 Nasuh, meanwhile,
has gone to his private closet, trembling.

"I didn't steal the pearl,
but if they undress and search me,
they'll see how excited I get
with these nude ladies.
                        God, please,
help me!
         I have been cold and lecherous,
but cover my sin this time, PLEASE!
Let me not be exposed for how I've been.
I'll repent!"
              He weeps and moans and weeps,
for the moment is upon him.
                            "Nasuh!
We have searched everyone but you. Come out!"

2

At that moment his spirit grows wings, and lifts.
His ego falls like a battered wall.
He unites with God, alive,
but emptied of
Nasuh.

His ship sinks and in its place move the ocean waves.
His body's disgrace, like a falcon's loosened binding,
slips from the falcon's foot.

His stones drink in Water.
His field shines like satin with gold threads in it.
Someone dead a hundred years steps out well
and strong and handsome.
                              A broken stick
breaks into bud.

This all happens inside Nasuh,
after the call that gave him such fear.

A long pause.
A long, waiting silence.

Then a shout from one of the women, "Here it is!"
The bathhouse fills with clapping.
Nasuh sees his new life sparkling out before him.

The women come to apologize, "We're so sorry
we didn't trust you. We just knew
that you'd taken that pearl."

They kept talking about how they'd suspected him,
and begging his forgiveness.

Finally he replies,

"I am much more guilty
than anyone has thought or said. I am the worst person
in the world. What you have said is only a hundredth
of what I've actually done. Don't ask my pardon!

You don't know me. No one knows me.
God has hidden my sneakiness. Satan taught me tricks,
but after a time, those became easy, and I taught Satan
some new variations. God saw what I did, but chose
not to publicly reveal my sin.

And now, I am sewn back into Wholeness!
Whatever I've done,
                              now was not done.
Whatever obedience I didn't do,
                                        now I did!
Pure, noble, free, like a cypress,
                                   like a lily,
is how I suddenly am. I said,
                              "Oh No!
Help me!"
                And that *Oh No!* became a rope
let down in my well. I've climbed out to stand here
in the sun. One moment I was at the bottom
of a dank, fearful narrowness, and the next,

I am not contained by this Universe.

If every tip of every hair on me could speak,
I still couldn't say my gratitude.

In the middle of these streets and gardens, I stand and say
and say again, and it's all I say,
                              "I wish everyone
could know what I know."

Some time later a messenger came to Nasuh,
"The young Princess would like for you to wash her hair.
She will let no one touch her but you."

Nasuh and the Princess had been very close,
but he replied,
                    "Nasuh is very sick. I've lost my touch.
Look for someone else to tend the women's hair.
I'm out of that business."

He thought to himself, "The cold way I was
still frightens me. In it, I tasted
a kind of bitter living-death,

but this new life is real. I will stay in its grace,
until my soul leaves my body."

One delight can only be replaced by a greater delight.
Nasuh found a Friend lovelier than the Princess.

(*Mathnawi*,V, 2228-2324, 2381)

Images of the Unseen

Is it right to make images
of how the Unseen world works?

Only the One who knows such things can do that.
How can our bald heads explain hair?

Moses thought what he saw was a stick,
but it had a dragon inside it.

If such a spiritual King
could not see inside a piece of wood,
how can we possibly understand temptation and destiny,
the grain thrown out and the Thrower's purposes?

We're mice peeking around
and meddling where we ought not.

The images we invent
could change into wild beasts
and tear us to pieces!

Satan said that He was fire and that Adam was clay,
and with that comparison he destroyed himself.

In Noah's time people mocked his shipbuilding
with metaphors.
                    "Maybe it will sprout legs
and walk away!"
                    "Put some wings on it!"

But Noah knew his work was right.
He didn't mind what they said.

Here's a story.

A thief was cutting a hole through the wall of a house
at night. The owner was sick and groggy,
but he heard the soft, digging tap of the pick.

He got up and climbed out on the roof
and hung his head over to look,
                                "What's going on down there?
Why are you out in the middle of the night?
Who are you?"
                "I'm a drummer, my friend."

"How wonderful. But I don't hear any drum music."
"You will.
                Tomorrow you'll hear a song that goes,

        Oh no! What has happened?

        Oh no! I've been robbed!"

This is how we sound
when we talk about spiritual matters,
saying "moon" and "soul" and "spirit guide."

What do we mean by these words?
Sometimes I say The Sun within the Sun inside the Sun,
and claim to be describing God.
                                I'm talking
in my sleep.

(*Mathnawi,* III, 2785-2804)

7

Two Ways of Running

A certain man has a jealous wife
and a very, very appealing maidservant.

The wife was careful not to leave them alone,
ever. For six years they were never left
in a room together.
                            But then one day
at the public bath the wife suddenly remembered
that she'd left her silver wash-basin at home.

"Please, go get the basin," she told her maid.

The girl jumped to the task, because she knew
that she would finally get to be alone
with the master. She ran joyfully.
                            She flew,
and desire took them both so quickly
that they didn't even latch the door.

With great speed they joined each other.
When bodies blend in copulation,
spirits also merge.

Meanwhile, the wife back at the bathhouse,
washing her hair, "What have I done!
I've set the cotton-wool on fire! I've put
the ram in with the ewe!"

She washed the clay soap off her hair and ran,
fixing her chadar about her as she went.

The maid ran for love. The wife ran out of fear

and jealousy. There is a great difference.

The mystic flies moment to moment.
The fearful ascetic drags along month to month.

But also the length of a "day" to a Lover
may be fifty thousand years!

You can't understand this with your mind.
You must burst open!

Fear is nothing to a Lover, a tiny piece of thread.
Love is a Quality of God. Fear is an attribute
of those who think they serve God, but who are actually
preoccupied with penis and vagina.

You have read in the text where *They love Him*
blends with *He loves them*.
                              Those joining Loves
are both Qualities of God. Fear is not.

What characteristics do God and human beings
have in common? What is the connection between
what lives in time and what lives in eternity?

If I kept talking about Love,
a hundred new combinings would happen,
and still I would not say the Mystery.

The fearful ascetic runs on foot, along the surface.
Lovers move like lightning and wind.
                              No contest.
Theologians mumble, rumble-dumble,
necessity and free will,
while lover and Beloved
                         pull themselves

into each other.

The worried wife reaches the door
and opens it.
          The maid, disheveled, confused, flushed,
unable to speak.
          The husband begins his five-times prayer.

The wife enters this agitated scene.
As though experimenting with clothes,
the husband holds up some flaps and edges.

She sees his testicles and penis so wet, semen
still dribbling out, spurts of gism and vaginal juices
drenching the thighs of the maid.
                    The wife slaps him
on the side of the head,
                    "Is this the way
a man prays, with his balls?
                    Does your penis
long for Union like this?
                    Is that why
her legs are so covered with this stuff?"

These are good questions
she's asking her "ascetic" husband!

People who renounce desires
often turn, suddenly,
into hypocrites!

(*Mathnawi*, V, 2163–2204, 2210)

10

In Baghdad, Dreaming of Cairo: In Cairo, Dreaming of Baghdad

No more muffled drums!
Uncover the drumheads!

Plant your flag in an open field!
No more timid peeking around.

Either you see the Beloved,
or you lose your head!

If your throat's not ready for that Wine, cut it!
If your eyes don't want the fullness of Union,
let them turn white with disease.

Either this deep desire of mine
will be found on this journey,
or when I get back home!

It may be that the satisfaction I need
depends on my going away, so that when I've gone
and come back, I'll find it at home.

I will search for the Friend with all my passion
and all my energy, until I learn
that I don't need to search.

The real truth of existence is sealed,
until after many twists and turns of the road.

As in the algebraical method of "the two errors,"
the correct answer comes only after two substitutions,
after two mistakes. Then the seeker says,

"If I had known the real way it was,
I would have stopped all the looking around."

But that knowing depends
on the time spent looking!

Just as the Sheikh's debt could not be paid
until the boy's weeping, that story we told in Book II.

You fear losing a certain eminent position.
You hope to gain something from that, but it comes
from elsewhere. Existence does this switching trick,
giving you hope from one source, then satisfaction
from another.
          It keeps you bewildered and wondering,
and lets your trust in the Unseen grow.

You think to make your living from tailoring,
but then somehow money comes in
through goldsmithing,
which had never entered your mind.

I don't know whether the Union I want will come
through my effort, or my giving up effort,
or from something completely separate
from anything I do or don't do.

I wait and fidget and flop about
as a decapitated chicken does, knowing that
the vital spirit has to escape this body
eventually, somehow!

This desire will find an opening.

There was once a man
who inherited a lot of money and land.

But he squandered it all too quickly. Those who inherit
wealth don't know what work it took to get it.

In the same way, we don't know the value of our souls,
which were given to us for nothing!

So the man was left alone without provisions,
an owl in the desert.
                    The Prophet has said
that a true seeker must be completely empty like a lute
to make the sweet music of *Lord, Lord.*

When the emptiness starts to get filled with something,
the One who plays the lute puts it down
and picks up another.

There is nothing more subtle and delightful
than to make that music.
                    Stay empty and held
between those fingers, where *where*
gets drunk with Nowhere.
                    This man was empty,
and the tears came. His habitual stubbornness
dissolved. This is the way with many seekers.
They moan in prayer, and the perfumed smoke of that
floats into Heaven, and the angels say, "Answer
this prayer. This worshiper has only You
and nothing else to depend on. Why do you go first
to the prayers of those less devoted?"
                    God says,
"By deferring My Generosity I am helping him.
His need dragged him by the hair into My Presence.
If I satisfy that, he'll go back to being absorbed
in some idle amusement. Listen how passionate he is!
That torn-open cry is the way he should live."

Nightingales are put in cages
because their songs give pleasure.
Whoever heard of keeping a crow?

When two people, one decrepit and the other young
and handsome, come into a bakery where the baker
is an admirer of young men, and both of them
ask for bread, the baker will immediately
give what he has on hand to the old man.

But to the other he will say, "Sit down and wait a while.
There's fresh bread baking in the house. Almost ready!"

And when the hot bread is brought, the baker will say,
"Don't leave. The halvah is coming!"

So he finds ways of detaining the young man with,
"Ah, there's something important I want to tell you about.
Stay. I'll be back in a moment. Something
very important!"

This is how it is when true devotees
suffer disappointment
in the good they want to do,
or the bad they want to avoid.

So this man with nothing, who had inherited everything
and squandered it, kept weeping, *Lord, Lord!*

Finally in a dream he heard a Voice, "Your wealth
is in Cairo. Go there to such and such a spot
and dig, and you'll find what you need."

So he left on the long journey,
and when he saw the towers of Cairo,
he felt his back grow warm with new courage.

14

But Cairo is a large city,
and before he could find the spot,
he had to wander about.

He had no money, of course, so he begged
among the townspeople, but he felt ashamed doing that.
He decided, "I will go out at night
and call like the night-mendicants that people
throw coins into the street for."
                              Shame and dignity and hunger
were pushing him forward and backward and sideways!

Suddenly, he was seized by the night-patrol.
It so happened that many had been robbed recently
in Cairo at night, and the Caliph had told the police
to assume that anyone out roaming after dark
was a thief.
                    It's best not to let offenders go unpunished.
Then they poison the whole body of society. Cut off
the snakebitten finger! Don't be sympathetic
with thieves. Consider instead
the public suffering. In those days
robbers were expert, and numerous!

So the night-patrol grabbed the man.
                                         "Wait!
I can explain!"
                  "Tell me."
                              "I am not a criminal.
I am new to Cairo. I live in Baghdad." And then
he told the story of his dream and the buried treasure,
and he was so believable in the telling that
the night-patrolman began to cry. Always,
the fragrance of Truth has that effect.
                                         Passion

15

can restore healing power, and prune the weary boughs
to new life. The energy of passion is everything!

There are fake satisfactions that simulate passion.
They taste cold and delicious,
but they just distract you and prevent you
from the search. They say,
                              "I will relieve your passion.
Take me. Take me!"
                              Run from false remedies
that dilute your energy. Keep it rich and musky.

The night-patrol said, "I know you're not a thief.
You're a good man, but you're kind of a fool.
I've had that dream before.

I was told, in my dream, that there was a treasure for me
in Baghdad, buried in a certain quarter of the city
on such-and-such a street."
                              The name of the street
that he said was where this man lived!
                              "And the dream-
voice told me, 'It's in So-and-so's house.
Go there and get it!'"

Without knowing either,
he had described the exact house,
and mentioned this man's name!

"But I didn't do what the dream said to do,
and look at you, who did, wandering the world,
fatigued, and begging in the streets!"
                              So it came quietly
to the seeker, though he didn't say it out loud,
"What I'm longing for
lived in my poor house in Baghdad!"

16

He filled with joy. He breathed continuous praise.
Finally he said,
    "The Water of Life is here.
I'm drinking it. But I had to come
this long way to know it!"

(*Mathnawi,* VI, 4167-4275, 4280, 4302-4319, 4324-
4326)

Dying, Laughing

A lover was telling his Beloved
how much he loved her, how faithful
he had been, how self-sacrificing, getting up
at dawn every morning, fasting, giving up
wealth and strength and fame,
all for her.

There was a fire in him.
He didn't know where it came from,
but it made him weep and melt like a candle.

"You've done well," she said, "but listen to me.
All this is the decor of love, the branches
and leaves and blossoms. You must live
at the root to be a True Lover."
                              "Where is that!
Tell me!"
          "You've done the outward acts,
but you haven't died. You must die."

When he heard that, he lay back on the ground
laughing, and died. He opened like a rose
that drops to the ground and died laughing.

That laughter was his freedom,
and his gift to the Eternal.

As moonlight shines back at the sun,
he heard the call to come home, and went.

When light returns to its Source,
it takes nothing

of what it has illuminated.

It may have shone on a garbage dump, or a garden,
or in the center of a human eye. No matter.

It goes, and when it does,
the open plain becomes passionately desolate,
wanting it back.

(*Mathnawi,* V, 1242-1264)

Human Honesty

They were outdoors in some sort of fake
spiritual state, the hypocrite
and his friend, the mayor.

It was midnight, and raining.
A wolf appeared on the edge of the hill.
The mayor let fly an arrow that felled the wolf,
who moaned and farted
and died.

The hypocrite yelled, "You've killed my donkey.
I know my donkey's farts as well as I know
water from wine."
                    "Not so. I shot a wolf.
Go and see. It's too dark to tell anything
from here."
                    "Among twenty farts from twenty animals,
I would know the wind from my young donkey.
Some things I know perfectly."
                    "You imposter!
In the rain, at midnight, at fifty yards,
you can distinguish one fart from another!
You didn't even recognize me today,
and we've know each other for ten years!

You're just pretending with this God-drunkenness too,
so you'll be excused for other forgetfulnesses,
as a child is, or someone who's truly dissolved
in that Joy. You're not. You're too proud
of your 'dervishhood,' and your cries
of 'selfless surrender.'
                    'O, both worlds are here!

I can't tell which is which! My donkey's farts
prove the sensitivity of my state!'"
                              This is the way
hypocrisy gets exposed. Anyone who claims,
"I am the Keeper of the Doorway," will be tested
by the Adepts, as when some guy claims to be a tailor
and the King throws down a piece of satin,
"Make me a vest."
                    The Wine God loves
is human honesty.
                    That hypocrite had been drinking
buttermilk. He was saying, "Leave me alone
in my bewilderment. I don't know a hatchet
from a key. I am Junaid. I am Bestami!"
Spiritual sloth and spiritual greed
will not stay hidden.

If you pretend to be Hallaj
and with that fake-burning
set fire to your friends,
don't think that you're a Lover.

You're crazy and numb.
You're drinking our blood,
and you have no experience
of the Nearness.

(*Mathnawi,* III, 650-702)

Dalqak's Message

The King of Tirmid
had urgent business in Samarcand.

He needed a courier to go there and return
in five days. He offered many rewards to anyone
who would make the journey—horses, servants, gold,
and the robes of honor.
                    Dalqak, the court clown,
was out in the country when he heard of this.
He quickly mounted a horse and rode toward town.
He rode furiously. Two horses dropped dead
of exhaustion under his whip.
                    He arrived
covered with dust at some ungodly hour,
demanding an audience with the King.

A panic swept the city. What calamity
could be imminent that Dalqak, the buffoon,
should be so distraught? Everyone gathered
at the palace.
                    "An evil omen is upon us!"
"Something has certainly been spilled on the rug
this time!"
                    The King himself was worried.
"What is it, Dalqak?"
                    Whenever anyone asked Dalqak
for particulars about anything, he first put his finger
to his lips,
                    Shhhhh.....
                    Everyone got very quiet.
Dalqak made another gesture as though to say

he needed more time to catch his breath.

Another long wait. No one had ever seen Dalqak
like this. Usually, he was a constant stream
of new jokes. Usually, the King would be
laughing so hard he'd fall on the floor
holding his stomach. This quietness
was very odd and foreboding.

        Everyone's worst fears
came up.
        "The tyrant from Khwarism
is coming to kill us!"
        "Dalqak, tell what it is!"

"I was far from the court when I heard
that you needed a courier, someone who could go
to Samarcand and come back in five days."
        "Yes!"
"I hurried here to tell you
that I will not be able to do it."
        "What!"
"I don't have the stamina or the agility.
Don't expect me to be the one."
        "This
is what you made such a commotion about,
that you won't do it?"
        This is like those who pretend
to be on a brave spiritual path.
        The bridegroom's house
is in an uproar of preparation, always making ready
to receive the bride,
        but the girl's family
knows nothing. Any message yet?
        "No."
Any sign of activity?
        "No."

Letters have been written
and sent, but have any of them reached
the Friend? Has your Inner
Lover read them?

(*Mathnawi,* VI, 2510-2554)

Faraj's Wedding Night

A certain King had a Hindu servant named Faraj,
whom he had educated, a very lively young man,
curious about the sciences and the arts.

The candle of his intellect had been lit,
and he was thriving in the King's kindness.

The King also had a beautiful daughter.
Her legs and arms were smooth and glowing
like silver. Her disposition, radiant.

She had almost reached the age of marriage,
and she had many suitors offering fabulous dowries.
Every day a new courtier came.

But this was a wise King, who thought to himself,
"Wealth means nothing. It blows in
on the morning breeze, and out
on the evening. And the same with physical beauty.
A handsome face can be scratched in the thorns.
And noble birth is also worthless. The children
of the nobility are usually interested only
in money and horses." And special talents too
are not what's truly valuable.

There is a kind of Knowing that is a love.
Not a scholarly knowing. That minutiae-collecting
doesn't open you. It inflates you, like a beard
or a fancy turban. It announces you, saying,

There are certain plusses and minuses
which we must carefully consider.

This other Knowing-Love is a rising light,
a happiness in both worlds. The King chose
for his daughter a husband with that Quality,
and everyone criticized him. "He has no wealth.
He's not handsome, and he's not from a famous line."

The King simply replied, "Those characteristics
are not important." The marriage was arranged,
and preparations began, but the Hindu servant, Faraj,
became sick and could do nothing.
He was dizzy and weak.
The doctors could not determine a cause.

One night the King said to his wife,
"You are like a mother to Faraj. Go to him
and see what's wrong." The next morning she went
and brushed Faraj's hair and kissed his cheek
and soothed him, until finally he told her
the secret, "I am in love with your daughter.
I never thought you would give her away
to someone else!"

The Queen could barely restrain her surprise
and her anger at this, but she did. "Be patient,"
was all she said, and then returned to the King.

"Can you imagine this presumptuous servant
thinking he would marry our daughter!"

"Don't scold him," said the King. "In fact,
he must be told that we will break off the engagement
and give our daughter to him. This news
will make him well! Animals are made strong
and happy by feeding them fodder. Young men
are made happy and physically active

by the expectation that their desires
for honors and for the girl they think they want
will soon be satisfied. So the young man was told,
and a party was held to celebrate how the King
had arranged a marriage for Faraj. Faraj strutted about
very full of health and new energy.

On the wedding night, though, the King sent a substitute,
an adolescent boy disguised in a dress
with fingernails painted and forearms decorated
like a girl's. That was all that showed
of this rough approximation of a bride!

At the customary hour, the excited husband was left alone
with this covered figure. The father quickly
blew out the candle and left.

There were some surprised cries,
but because of the noisy music,
no one outside the chamber
heard anything.

The drum and the tambourine kept beating.
The hands kept clapping.
The cries of the men and the women outside
blended with the cries of the two adolescents inside.

Came the dawn. Faraj and the disguised one
were tangled in an embrace. What does a dog
know of a sack of flour? As is the way,
clean clothes were brought. Very confused, Faraj
gets up and goes to bathe. Troubled and torn, shredded
to his very basis, like the rags of the bath-stokers,
Faraj returns to find the actual girl seated
in the marriage chamber with her mother.

He eyes them both for a long while,
then holds up both hands and waves them away.

"May no one ever be cursed with such a wife!
In the daytime, you're beautiful, but at night
your private parts are deformed
and worse than a donkey's!"

This is true of all world-pleasures.
They look delightful before you test them out.
The world looks like a delicate bride,
but be more patient than Faraj!

The eminence you think you want, the power
over others, let all that go.

It's better not to ride on other people's backs.
That's how we arrive at the grave.
Tend just to what's yours.

If you drop your whip, dismount, and pick it up.
Don't ask someone else to do your work.

Ask within, and when that Presence directs you,
whatever you do will be right, even though
externally it may seem wrong. Don't curse the oyster
for having an ugly, encrusted shell. Inside,
it's all pearl. There's no way to ever say
how we are with phenomena.

Like a moth with a candle, we singe our wings
and then forget and come back to do the same thing.

Like children, we spill the salt,
and then we spill it again.

Like Faraj, we put up both hands and say, "No!
Your face is very lovely, but in bed
you're something totally different.
I won't be fooled again!"

But he will. We make resolutions,
and we forget. Paper flares up,
and then goes out.

(*Mathnawi,*VI, 249-356)

Bestami

That magnificent dervish, Bayazid Bestami,
came to his disciples and said,
                              "I am God."
It was night, and he was drunk with his ecstasy.
"There is no God but me. You should worship me."

At dawn, when he had returned to normal,
they came and told him what he'd said.
                              "If I say that again,
bring your knives and plunge them into me. God
is beyond the body, and I am in this body.
Kill me when I say that."
                              Each student then sharpened
his knife, and again Bayazid drank the God-Wine.
The sweet dessert-knowing came. The Inner Dawn
snuffed his candle. Reason, like a timid advisor,
faded to a far corner as the Sun-Sultan
entered Bayazid.
                              Pure spirit spoke through him.
Bayazid was not there. The "he" of his personality
dissolved. Like the Turk who spoke fluent Arabic,
then came to, and didn't know a word.
                              The Light of God
poured into the empty Bayazid and became words.

Muhammed did not dictate the *Qur'an*. God did.
The mystic osprey opened its wings in Bayazid
and soared.
                              "Inside my robe
there is nothing but God.
How long will you keep looking elsewhere!"

The disciples drew their knifes and slashed out
like assassins, but as they stabbed at their Sheikh,
they did not cut Bayazid. They cut themselves.

There was no mark on that Adept,
but the students were bleeding and dying.

Those who somewhat held back, respecting their Teacher,
had only lightly wounded themselves.
                                        A selfless One
disappears into Existence and is safe there.
He becomes a mirror. If you spit at it,
you spit at your own face.

If you see an ugly face there, it's yours.
If you see Jesus and Mary, they're you.

Bayazid became nothing,
that clear and that empty.

A saint puts your image before you.
When I reach this point, I have to close my lips.

Those of you who are love-drunk on the edge of the roof,
sit down, or climb down. Every moment spent in Union
with the Beloved is a dangerous delight,
like standing on a roof-edge.
                              Be afraid up there,
of losing that connection, and don't tell anybody
about it. Keep your secret.

(*Mathnawi,* IV, 2102-2148)

Eyes-Shut Facing Eyes-Rolling-Around

Pay close attention to your mean thoughts.

That sourness may be a blessing,
as an overcast day brings rain for the roses
and relief to dry soil.

Don't look so sourly on your sourness!
It may be it's carrying what you most deeply need
and want. What seems to be keeping you from joy
may be what leads you to joy.

Don't call it a dead branch.
Call it the live, moist root.

Don't always be waiting to see
what's behind it. That wait and see
poisons your Spirit.

Reach for it.
Hold your meanness to your chest
as a healing root,
and be through with waiting.

The Sultan Mahmud said to Ayaz,
"Your sincerity does not waver
in your moments of lust or anger.
This stability is true virility.
Without it, a king is just
a donkey's fart!"
              The *Qur'an* has said
what men really are. Where does the animal-soul
figure into that?

Come. Walk with me
through the butchershop. See the sheepheads
lying on top of the sections of tripe.

The heads are worth less than the fatty tailbone
and the tail. They are like the woman who,
at the push of a penis, lost her clear intellect
and became a blind animal.
                       There was once a wise man
who had a beautiful daughter with a lovely face
and perfect breasts. When she reached maturity,
he gave her in marriage to a husband who was not
an appropriate match for her.
                       When a melon gets ripe,
you must slice it, or it gets watery and inedible.

He tells his daughter, "Do not get pregnant.
This man is a wanderer. He will leave you,
at any moment, to raise the child alone."

"Father, I value your wisdom,
and I'll do as you say."

Every two or three days the father came
and reminded his daughter of the precautions
she should be taking. Nevertheless,
she got pregnant. How could it happen otherwise
when a wife and a husband are young?

She had the child and somehow kept it hidden
from her father for five or six months.
Then he saw it.
                "What's this! Didn't I tell you
how to pull back from your husband?"
                       "Yes, father,
but how am I to do that? A man and a woman

are like a flame and a piece of cotton.
Can the cotton keep itself from catching fire?"
The father replied,
        "Don't move toward him to receive
his semen. At the delicious peak-time, be sure
you draw back away from him."
        "But how can I know
when his emission is coming? This is hidden,
and difficult to know, exactly."
        The father replied,
"When he's pushing hard at you, with his eyes
rolling around, that's the crucial time."
        "But father,
while his eyes are doing that, mine are sealed shut!"

So, like that, not every understanding can remain clear
during the entanglement-times of desire and anger.

There was once a Sufi who, when the others went out
to battle, he stayed behind in the tents
with the heavy baggage and the invalids.
The light-footed warriors rode off
and came back with trophies.

They gave him a present from the battle,
but he threw it out of the tent.
        "Why are you angry?"
"I did not take part in the Holy War.
I have been kept out of the action,
and I will not accept anything from it."

"We have brought back some prisoners,
who must be executed. Take one, and cut off his head,
and then you'll be a Holy Warrior like the rest of us."

The cowardly Sufi thought, "Yes,

that's like the injunction,
If you don't have water for ablutions, use sand."

So he led the prisoner behind the tent
to wage his Holy War.

He was back there a long time.
The soldiers began wondering, "The prisoner
had his hands tied behind him, and he was ready to die,
yet this dervish is taking so long!"

One of them went to investigate and found the prisoner
on top of the Sufi like a man on top of a woman,
like a lion on an antelope gnawing the neck.

The infidel was biting the unconscious Sufi on the neck!
His beard was soaked with the dervish's blood.

This is an image of those of you
who have let your animal-soul, although bound
by many religious laws, still you've let it
get on top of you. You and your religious restrictions
lie stunned beneath that fierce animal.

The soldiers immediately slew the prisoner
and sprinkled rosewater on the Sufi
to wake him up. He came to.
      "That man!
As I was about to behead him, he looked straight
at me, and then he rolled his eyes around so wildly
that I fainted."
     The soldiers could not believe it.
They advised him,
      "Don't even think of going to battle.
You'll see eyes there that consider your head
no more than a polo ball, and you'll see headless

35

bodies spilling into the mud, and there won't be
anyone there to revive you when you faint
with a sip of wheat-broth!

Such things are not for easily-fading,
feminine beings.
                              Stay home.
Let the iron warriors of Muhammed
do the fighting-work."

(*Mathnawi*, V, 3696-3779)

The Visions of Daquqi

Husam,
tell about the visions of Daquqi,
who said,
      "I have traveled east and west not knowing
which way I was going, following the moon,
lost inside God."
      Someone asked, "Why do you go bare-
footed over the stones and thorns?"
      "What," he answered.
"What."
      A bewildered Lover doesn't walk on feet.
He or she walks on Love. There are no "long"
or "short" trips for those. No time.

The body learned from the spirit how to travel.
A saint's body moves in the unconditioned way,
though it seems to be in conditionedness.

Daquqi said,
      "One day I was going along
looking to see in people the shining of the Friend,
so I would recognize the ocean in a drop,
the sun in a bright speck.
      I came to the shore
at twilight and saw seven candles. I hurried
along the beach toward them. The light of each
lifted into the sky. I was amazed. My amazement
was amazed. Waves of bewilderment
broke over my head.

What are these candles that no one seems to see?
In the Presence of such lights people were looking

for lamps to buy!
                    Then the seven became one,
in the middle of the sky's rim.
                    Then that
fanned out to seven again. There were connections
between the candles that cannot be said.
I saw, but I cannot say.

I ran closer. I fell. I lay there awhile.
I got up and ran again. I had no head and no feet.

They became seven men, and then seven trees,
so dense with leaves and fruit
that no limbs were visible.
                    Flashes of light
spurted from each fruit like juice!

And most marvelous of all was that hundreds
of thousands of people were passing beside the trees,
risking their lives, sacrificing everything,
to find some scrap of shade.
                    They made peculiar parasols
out of pieces of wool. They tried anything.

And no one saw the trees with their tremendous shade!
The caravans had no food, and yet food was dropping
all about them. If anyone had said,
                    'Look! Over here!'
they would have thought him insane, or drunk.

How can this happen? Or am I dreaming?
I walk up to the trees. I eat the fruit.
I might as well believe.
                    And still I see people
searching so desperately for an unripe grape,
with these vineyards around them,

heavy with perfect bunches.

Then the seven trees became one, and then seven again.
At every second they were both seven and one.

They were doing the ritual prayer, kneeling and bowing,
without knees or waists!
                              Then they were seven men
seated in meditation for the sake of the One Reality.

I came closer and waved. They called,
                              'O Daquqi,
the glory and the crown!'
                              'How do they know my name?'
I thought. 'They've never seen me till now.'

Immediately they knew my thought,
and smiled at each other.
                              'Honored one,
is this still hidden from you? How can anything
be hidden from one so dissolved in God?'

'If this is the spirit-reality,' I said to myself,
'how is it we're speaking words and saying names.'

One of the seven answered, 'Names.
Sometimes the names slip away from us,
but it's not forgetfulness.
It's our being so absorbed.'

Then they all said to me,
'Would you lead us in prayer?'
                              'Yes. But wait awhile.
I am still in some temporal confusion
that will be solved by companionship with you.

Through companionship with the ground a grapevine
grows. It opens into the earth's darkness
and flies. It becomes selfless
in the presence of its origin and learns
what it really is.'
                    They nodded, as though saying,
'Whenever you're ready.' That nodding
was a flame in my heart.
                    I was freed from hourly time,
from sequence and relation."

                    Everyone has a stable
and a trainer appointed to him or her. If you break away,
the trainer comes and gets you. You think
you're making choices, but the trainer is actually
leading you around.
                    You like to deny
that you have a keeper. You say,
                    "It's my powerful
animal urges."

(*Mathnawi,* III, 1972-2029, 2046-2083)

Sexual Urgency, What A Woman's Laughter Can Do, and The Nature of True Virility

Someone offhand to the Caliph of Egypt:
"The King of Mosul
has a concubine like no other,
more beautiful than I can describe.
She looks like *this*."
He draws her likeness on paper.

The Caliph drops his cup.
Immediately he sends his Captain to Mosul
with an army of thousands. The siege goes on for a week,
with many casualties, the walls and the towers unsteady,
as soft as wax. The King of Mosul sends an envoy:
"Why this killing? If you want the city,
I will leave and you can have it!
If you want more wealth, that's even easier."

The Captain takes out the piece of paper
with the girl's picture on it. This.
The strong King of Mosul is quick to reply.
"Lead her out. The idol belongs with the idolater."

When the Captain sees her, he falls in love
like the Caliph. Don't laugh at this.
This loving is also part of infinite Love,
without which the world does not evolve.
Objects move from inorganic to vegetation
to selves endowed with spirit through the urgency
of every love that wants to come to perfection.

This Captain thinks the soil looks fertile,
so he sows his seed. Sleeping, he sees the girl
in a dream. He makes love to her image,

and his semen spurts out.

After a while he begins to wake.
Slowly he senses the girl is not there.
"I have given my seed into nothing.
I shall put this tricky woman to a test."

A leader who is not captain of his body is not one
to be honored, with his semen spilled so in the sand.
Now he loses all control. He doesn't care
about the Caliph, or about dying.
"I am in love," he says.

Do not act in such heat.
Take counsel with a Master.
But the Captain couldn't.

His infatuation is a blackwater wave carrying him away.
Something that doesn't exist makes a phantom
appear in the darkness of a well,
and the phantom itself becomes strong enough
to throw actual lions into the hole.

More advice: It is dangerous to let other men
have intimate connections with the women in your care.
Cotton and fire-sparks, those are, together.
Difficult, almost impossible, to quench.

The Captain does not return straight to the Caliph,
but instead camps in a secluded meadow.
Blazing, he can't tell ground from sky.
His reason is lost in a drumming sound,
worthless radish and son of a radish.
The Caliph himself a gnat, nothing.

But just as this cultivator tears off the woman's pants

and lays down between her legs, his penis
moving straight to the mark, there's a great tumult
and a rising cry of soldiers outside the tent.
He leaps up with his bare bottom shining
and runs out, scimitar in hand.

A black lion from a nearby swamp
has gotten in among the horses. Chaos.
The lion jumping twenty feet in the air,
tents billowing like an ocean.

The Captain quickly approaches the lion,
splits his head with one blow,
and now he's running back to the woman's tent.
When he stretches out her beauty again,
his penis goes even more erect.

The engagement, the coming together, is as with the lion.
His penis stays erect all through it,
and it does not scatter semen feebly.
The beautiful one is amazed at his virility.
Immediately, with great energy she joins with his energy,
and their two spirits go out from them as one.

Whenever two are linked this way, there comes another
from the Unseen world. It may be through birth,
if nothing prevents conception,
but a third does come, when two unite in love,
or in hate. The intense qualities born
of such joining appear in the spiritual world.

You will recognize them when you go there.
Your associations bear progeny.
Be careful, therefore. Wait, and be conscious,
before you go to meet anyone.
Remember there are children to consider!

Children you must live with and tend to,
born of your emotions with another, entities
with a form, and speech, and a place to live.
They are crying to you even now.
You have forgotten us. Come back.
Be aware of this. A man and a woman together
always have a spiritual result.

The Captain was not so aware. He fell,
and stuck like a gnat in a pot of buttermilk,
totally absorbed in his love affair. Then,
just as suddenly, he's uninterested. He tells
the woman, "Don't say a word of this to the Caliph."

He takes her there, and the Caliph is smitten.
She's a hundred times more beautiful than he's imagined.

A certain man asks an eloquent teacher,
"What is true and what false?" "This is false:
A bat hides from the sun, not from the idea of the sun.
It's the idea that puts fear in the bat and leads it
deeper into the cave. You have an idea
of an enemy that attaches you to certain companions.

Moses, the inner light of revelation,
lit up the top of Sinai, but the mountain
could not hold that light.

Don't deceive yourself that way!
Having the idea is not living
the reality, of anything.

There's no courage in the idea of battle.
The bathhouse wall is covered with pictures

and much talk of heroism. Try to make an idea move
from ear to eye. Then your woolly ears
become as subtle as fibres of light.

Your whole body becomes a mirror,
all eye and spiritual breathing.
Let your ear lead you to your lover."

So the Caliph is mightily in love with this girl.
His kingdom vanishes like lightning.
If your loving is numb, know this: When what you own
can vanish, it's only a dream, a vanity, breath
through a mustache. It would have killed you.

There are those that say, "Nothing lasts."
They're wrong. Every moment they say,
"If there were some other reality,
I would have seen it. I would know about it."

Because a child doesn't understand a chain of reasoning,
should adults give up being rational?
If reasonable people don't feel the presence of love
within the universe, that doesn't mean it's not there.

Joseph's brothers did not see Joseph's beauty,
but Jacob never lost sight of it. Moses at first
saw only a wooden staff, but to his other seeing
it was a viper and a cause of panic.
Eye-sight is in conflict with inner knowing.
Moses' hand is a hand and a source of light.

These matters are as real as the infinite is real,
but they seem religious fantasies to some,
to those who believe only in the reality
of the sexual organs and the digestive tract.

Don't mention the Friend to those.
To others, sex and hunger are fading images,
and the Friend is more constantly, solidly here.
Let the former go to their church, and we'll go to ours.
Don't talk long to skeptics or to those
who claim to be atheists.

So the Caliph has the idea
of entering the beautiful woman,
and he comes to her to do his wanting.

Memory raises his penis, straining it in thought
toward the pushing down and the lifting up
which make that member grow large with delight.

But as he actually lays down with the woman,
there comes to him a decree from God
to stop these voluptuous doings. A very tiny sound,
like a mouse might make. The penis droops,
and desire slips away.

He thinks that whispering sound is a snake
rising off the straw mat. The girl sees his drooping
and sails into fits of laughing at the marvelous thing.
She remembers the Captain killing the lion
with his penis standing straight up.

Long and loud her laughter.
Anything she thinks of only increases it,
like the laughter of those who eat hashish.
Everything is funny.

Every emotion has a source and a key that opens it.
The Caliph is furious. He draws his sword.
"What's so amusing? Tell me everything you're thinking.
Don't hold anything back. At this moment

I'm clairvoyant. If you lie, I'll behead you.
If you tell the truth, I'll give you your freedom."

He stacks seven *Qur' ans* on top of each other
and swears to do as he says.
When she finally gets hold of herself
the girl tells all, in great detail. Of the camp
in the meadow, the killing of the lion,
the Captain's return to the tent with his penis
still hard as the horn of a rhino.

And the contrast with the Caliph's own member
sinking down because of one mouse-whisper.
Hidden things always come to light.
Do not sow bad seed. Be sure, they'll come up.
Rain and the sun's heat make them rise into the air.
Spring comes after the fall of the leaves,
which is proof enough of the fact of resurrection.
Secrets come out in Spring, out from earth-lips into leaf.
Worries become wine-headaches.
But where did the wine come from? Think.

A branch of blossoms does not look like seed.
A man does not resemble semen. Jesus came
from Gabriel's breath, but he is not in that form.
The grape doesn't look like the vine.
Loving actions are the seed of something
completely different, a living-place.
No origin is like where it leads to.
We can't know where our pain is from.
We don't know all that we've done.
Perhaps it's best that we don't.
Nevertheless we suffer for it.

The Caliph comes back to his clarity. "In the pride
of my power I took this woman from another,

47

so of course, someone came to knock on my door.
Whoever commits adultery is a pimp
for his own wife.

If you cause injury to someone, you draw
that same injury toward yourself. My treachery
made my friend a traitor to me. This repetition
must stop somewhere. Here, in an act of mercy.

I'll send you back to the Captain,
saying another of my wives is jealous,
and since the Captain was brave enough
to bring you back from Mosul,
he shall have you in marriage."

This is the virility of a prophet.
The Caliph was sexually impotent,
but his manliness was most powerful.

The kernel of true manhood is the ability
to abandon sensual indulgences. The intensity
of the Captain's libido is less than a husk
compared to the Caliph's nobility in ending
the cycle of sowing lust and reaping
secrecy and vengefulness.

(*Mathnawi,* V, 3831-4034)

The Court Poet

A poet brought a poem to the King
in hopes of wealth and the robes of honor.

The King was impressed, and generous
in his response. He awarded the poet
a thousand dinars of red gold.

But the King's advisor, Hasan, said,
"That is not enough. In such a fine poet
Intelligence Itself becomes visible,
and in a spiritual king like yourself
God's Oceanic Generosity should be revealed.
Give more!"
                    He argued and talked philosophy
and theology with the King in his chamber,
until the entire matter was threshed and sorted
like piles of corn on the threshing floor,
with a healthy tithing pile set to one side
for the poet, ten thousand dinars,
and the robes of honor!
                    "Who did this?"
asked the poet. "Who put my case so powerfully
to the King?"
                    "It was Hasan, which means *good,*
and he certainly is."

The poet wrote another poem for Hasan
and then returned home, while without words
the robes were praising the King's munificence.

After several years the poet fell on difficult times.
No food and no seed-grain, no means of growing food.

He thought,
          "When poverty gets acute, it's best to go
where one has gone before and found relief."

A famous saint once said
that the meaning of the Name of Allah is,
that worshipers should take refuge there.
In times of sudden danger all people call out, *O my God!*

Why would they keep doing this, if it didn't help?
Only a fool keeps going back where nothing happens.

The whole world lives within a safeguarding: fish
inside waves, birds held in the sky, the elephant,
the wolf, the lion as he hunts, the dragon, the ant,
the waiting snake, even the ground, the air,
water, every spark floating up from the fire,
all subsist, exist, in God. Nothing
is ever alone for a single moment.

All giving comes from There, no matter who
you think you put your open hand out
toward, it's That which gives.

So the poet went back a second time
with a new poem honoring the King.
Kings love praise.

The first human wanting is for food.
Then, as sometimes happens, when food is no longer
a worry, a person wants fame and the praise
of eloquent poets, wants a munificence
of song to float like perfume
over his or her life.

The Creator also wants glorification!

So it's built-in to the Essence of human beings
to want praise.

A strong leather bag fills with wind and shines
in the fullness of being praised.
A weaker, damaged, leather bag tears
and flaps dully in the same wind.

Friend, I have not made up this analogy.
Don't disregard it! Muhammed himself
said something similar when asked why
he got so happy when he was honored.

So the poet came to the King again saying,
"Givers die, but acts of generosity live on."

This is another topic.
Let it go.

The poet waits at the King's door
with his new poem. The King reads it, marveling.
"A thousand dinars to this poet."

The King's new advisor, also named Hasan—
the former Hasan had died—says, "We cannot afford
that much. A poet will be satisfied
with a fortieth of that."

"But," say others around the King,
"the last time he received ten thousand!"

"Let me explain it to him," said the new minister.
"I can handle these matters."

He tells the poet to come back later,
that the funding would be settled "in December."

In December, he says "Spring, perhaps in the spring."
The expectation lengthens, with the poet
becoming more and more desperate.
                                    "Soon,
he'll be grateful for a handful of road-dirt,"
thinks the minister.
                      Finally, the poet, "Please,
if there's to be nothing for me, don't lead me on.
This anticipation is killing me. It's like
being slowly tied up tighter and tighter."

Some courtiers take him aside,
                              "Accept this from us
and go. This new man is bitter and querulous.
It's best not to have any dealings with him. "

"What's his name?"
                  "Hasan."
                          "I can't believe it.
Two such opposites! One so giving,
and from the other's ugly beard
ropes are woven to tie up the poor,
so they'll be poorer."
                      The poet goes home
with his pittance.
                  This is the mystery:
The same generous King, the same
eloquent poet, but different
intermediary ministers,
                        with the same name!
Mean-spirited advisors
do sudden and shattering damage
to human structures.

(*Mathnawi,* IV, 1156-1244)

Spiritual Seniority

A camel and an ox and a ram
were ambling along a road, when they saw
a fresh tuft of barley grass
that they all wanted.

They stopped, and the ram said, "If we divide this,
none of us will be satisfied. Let us do
as Muhammed advised and give it to the eldest,
honoring his superior experience.

No one honors their elders these days
without some ulterior motive. The young
invite them to taste the food first
only when they suspect it's too hot.

They invite them to cross the bridge ahead of them
only when they see dangerous cracks in the arches,
and no one bows to a Teacher in these times
without some scam in mind. So let us each
declare his age and settle this matter.

As for me, I don't know my exact years,
but I was once pastured with that ram
that Abraham sacrificed instead of Isaac."

The ox, "Well, I can beat that! I was yoked
in the team that Adam plowed with when he left Eden."

The camel listened silently to their amazing lies,
reached his long neck down, plucked the luscious tuft,
and as he held it over their heads and ate it,
he said, "I don't know much about this chronology,

sweethearts, but I know I'm taller than you two, and that has obvious spiritual significance."

(*Mathnawi*, VI, 2457-2463, 2474-2483)

The Law Student and the Shroud-Maker

Nothing happens until you quit contriving
with your mind. Quit your talking.

Consider the story of Sadri Jahan of Bukhara,
who was very generous with beggars.
He wrapped pieces of gold in bits of paper
and gave them away as the sun and the moon
gamble their light trying to let go quickly
of the radiance given them.

Every morning Jahan chose a different set of people.
One day it might be the sick. Another, the widows,
or the law students, the ordinary country people,
or those in debt. Everybody had a turn
to receive Jahan's gold.
He only had one rule:
                        You mustn't ask out loud.

When he walked out, the mendicants stood
like silent walls on either side of his path.

If anyone made a begging sound to get his attention,
the punishment was *no alms,* ever again.
His motto was,

BLESSED ARE THE SILENT.

One day a wandering beggar blurted out suddenly,
"Please sir, I'm hungry."
                        Sadri Jahan turned,
"Have you no shame, old man?"
                        Quickly came the reply,

"Ah, but you're more shameless than I, Jahan."
                                            "How?"
"You enjoy this world, and in your greed for giving
you try to bring the other world here
to enjoy that one too."

Sadri Jahan laughed and gave him money,
but except for that one instance, he never gave
to those who spoke when he went by.
                                        Another day,
it was the poor law students. One of them
began a little involuntary whining noise
as Jahan approached. Jahan heard and noted
the impatience, and the punishment began.

The next day the law student put splints on his legs
and wrapped them in rags and stood among the crippled
with his head down. But Jahan recognized him.

The next day he put on a woman's robe and tried to mix
with the widows, totally veiled, but Jahan somehow
knew which outstretched hand *not* to put alms in.

In desperation the student went to a shroud-maker.
"Wrap me in black felt and set me out on the road.
When Jahan comes by, say nothing.
Just sit beside me, and anything he gives,
I'll split it with you."
                            So there they were,
the student lying wrapped in his shroud,
and the other beside him.

Jahan paused and dropped some gold pieces
on the shroud. The dead man's hand shot out to grab it,
so the shroud-maker wouldn't run off with the take.

He unwrapped himself and raised his head.
                                        "See Jahan,
I found a way back into your generosity."
                                        "Yes,
but you had to die to do it."
                        Here is the mystery
of *Die before you die.* Favors come
only after you develop the skill of dying,
and even that capacity is a mystical favor.

Be silent and wait,
and when the clear, green forehead-stone
is given, wear it.

(*Mathnawi,* VI, 3798-3842)

The Trick of Hiding in a Box

This world is a small piece of brocade,
a preposterous frontispiece at the beginning
of a wonderful book.
                              Anyone who believes this place
is all there is, let him or her be called,
"King of the World!" or "Queen of the World!"

O Body! You have enslaved so many free men
and women for so long! Quit plotting for a moment.
Be free from yourself for a little while
before you die.

Or if you're like a heavily loaded donkey,
or an old well-bucket, with no way to go but down,
then leave my spirit alone!
                              Find some other companion.
I'm finished playing your games. Beguile somebody else.
Say goodbye to me. You've taken almost my entire life.
Find some other victim.
                              Which reminds me of the story
of Juhi and his wife. Every year when they got poor,
Juhi would turn to his wife and say,
                              "Sweetheart,
you still have your traps and lures intact. Go out,
and catch us some game. Lay snares for a big bird!
Show the bait, but withhold it. Let him know
what he wishes for, but disappoint him. Let him
look at what he wanted from inside the trap!"

So his wife went to the local judge. "Sir, my husband
will not support me as he should. He doesn't give me
what I need."

58

That's the way she began, and to cut the story
short, the judge was hooked by her flirtatious ways.
He leaned to her,
            "There's too much commotion
in this courtroom. If you could meet me at my house,
then we could discuss in detail how your husband
has mistreated you."
            The young wife replied,
"But I'm sure that there, as here, there'll be a constant
coming and going of people who want to talk with you."

When the house of the brain fills with a wanting,
your heart gets crowded with anxieties.
The rest of the body may be undisturbed,
but in your chest there's constant traffic.

Find a safe haven instead
in the strong autumn wind of awe.
Let last year's peonies blow off their stems.
Those flowers must go, so these new buds can grow.

It's for the sake of new growth
that the tree of the heart exists.
Put your vanity to rest. Sleep and escape,
and wake within a new wakefulness,
like the Cave-sleepers, who were deeply awake,
though they seemed not to be.
                    Back to the judge
and the young wife.
                    "What shall we do, sweet one?"
"We could go to my house. No one is there.
My husband has gone to the country.
It'll be very private. Come at night.
No one will see you. Come when everyone's asleep
as though they'd drunk too much wine, dead-asleep
as though they'd been beheaded by the huge,

black executioner, Night."
                              The judge watched her lips
move as she said all this. Such excitement
she wove around him!
                         Women can do this
very easily. Satan often talked cunningly
with Adam, but only when Eve told him to eat,
did he eat. And Cain's violence
was caused by a woman too.

And remember Noah's wife.
She was always undermining his words of prophecy.
He'd be frying some meat, and she'd slip stones
into the skillet. She sent secret messages
to people,
              "Don't let this man influence you.
He's mistaken." The infinite guile of women!

So the wise judge came at night
to make love with Juhi's wife.
                              She had set the table
with two candles, a sweet dessert, and wine.

"I can do without these," he said. "I am already drunk
with wanting you."
                     At that moment Juhi knocked
on the door, his own door! The judge looked for a place
to hide. There was only an old chest.
He climbed in, trembling.

Enter Juhi. "O wife, why are you always complaining?
I have sacrificed everything for you, but still
you call me a pauper and a cuckold.
                                   The latter
is your fault, and the former comes from existence.
I own nothing now but this chest, which has, indeed,

60

become a source of suspicion in the community.
People think it's full of gold,
and so no one will give me any charity.

It is an attractive piece, isn't it?
But it's quite empty, believe me. In fact,
it's a perfect metaphor for hypocrisy.
Handsome and dignified outside,
but a snake within.
                        Tomorrow, I'll carry it out
into the middle of the bazaar and publicly burn it,
so that everyone can see that nothing was in it,
except that common cause for cursing,
nothing."
            "No!" cried the wife,
"There's no need for that!"
                        But Juhi was determined.
He repeated his plan several times.

Early the next morning he hired a porter
to carry the chest, and as the porter
was going along, the judge decided
it was time to act.
                "Porter! O Porter!"
The man looked right and left.
                        "Is this the Voice of
God, or is a genii calling to me?"
                More shouts in quick succession.
"This is not a revelation. This is coming
from inside the chest."
                A lover of world-things
has put himself in just such a box.
Though he appears to be free, he can see nothing
but the inside of his chosen chest.
He moves from tomb to tomb.
                        There's no end

61

to this subject!

The judge said,
            "Go tell the court deputy
to come and buy this chest and take it,
unopened, to the judge's house.
                  Lord,
appoint such powerful helpers to get us
out of our body-boxes!
                  No one but the prophets
and the saints can do that. Among thousands,
there are only a few who even know
that they are trapped inside a chest.
Such a one gets a glimpse of the spiritual world.

He recognizes his own lost camel,
and now he's certain where to go.

But some have never felt the delights of freedom.
They know only the dark box of phenomena.
The move from cage to cage.

In the *Qur'an* it says, "If you have power,
pass beyond."
                  It also says, "There is no way to do this
except through Divine Inspiration."

There is a pleasure in going from chest to chest,
a kind of stupefying novelty,
but there comes a time for some when,
like the judge, they want out.

The sign of one of those is the urgency of the weeping.

The deputy came to the market
where the chest had been brought.

"How much do you want for it?"
                         Juhi answered,
"They're offering nine hundred gold dinars,
but I can't go lower than a thousand.
Do you have that much?"
                         "Have you no shame
in your short felt tunic? The chest is obviously
not worth that much!"
                         Juhi replied, "Well,
maybe you're right, and it's certainly wrong
to be buying something in the dark.
I'll open the chest, and if it's not worth
what I'm asking, don't buy it."
                         The deputy quickly insisted,
"Keep the lid on. I want to buy it as is."

The haggling continued for a while longer.
Finally, the chest was sold to the court deputy
for a hundred dinars, and the judge was lugged home.

Those of you who find your wickedness pleasant,
it's like you're silently in your chest,
while spirit-voices outside argue,
trying to redeem you and let you out.

A year after this,
Juhi and his wife were again down to nothing.
"Clever wife, let's trick the judge one more time!"

She went to the courtroom with some other women,
heavily veiled, and remaining quiet,
so he wouldn't recognize her.

But, despite her coquettish looks,
she could not tempt the judge this time.

63

A woman's fascination is multiplied a hundred times
by the sound of her voice.

         "Go and bring the defendant here,"
demanded the judge.

         Juhi arrived, and of course,
the judge didn't recognize him. He had never seen him.
They had only met when he was in the chest.

But the judge had heard the bickering about the price.
"Why don't you support your wife as you should?"

"I am deeply devoted to religious law,
but I don't have money enough now to buy a shroud.
I'm broke, so I'll have to just play these cards I have."

Hearing the voice, the judge identified the tricksters
from a year ago.

         "I think we've dealt this hand
before, and the last time you bluffed me.
Try that bluff on someone else!
Get out of here, both of you."

The God-Knower cannot be fooled the same way twice.
He's out of the hexagonal well,
this up-and-down, left-right,
front-back container.

He lowers a bucket to draw out Joseph.
His body is the bucket that can rescue.
Other buckets go down for water.
His bucket goes for friends in trouble.

Other buckets are connected to the well-pulley
of Chance. His is held by God's fingers.

What bucket? What pulley? What rope?

There's no way a metaphor can say this.
There is no true comparison. All images
are hopelessly weak when it comes
to saying,
        You did not throw when you threw.

A hundred million sheaf-stacks
in one handful of grain.
A million men in one man.
Hundreds of bows and arrows
in a single peashooter.

A clod of dirt opens its mouth. The Sun's inside it!
Body, wash your hands in this Spirit.
The Ocean sloshes in this waterbag.
Jesus is inside this donkey!
A thousand Kaabas in one little country church!
A spaceless Object lives in space!

Many people ask, "How can I make a form of my love?"

A True Human Being is never what he or she
appears to be. Rub your eyes,
and look again.

(*Mathnawi,* VI, 4442-4525, 4536-4537, 4553-4588)

65

Berouged Old Ladies

There was a ninety-year-old woman,
her face wrinkled and yellowed, the folds as deep
as those in a desert-traveler's food wallet,
yet still she wanted to entice a husband.

Her teeth were gone, her hair milk-white,
She was bent over like a strung bow.
Her senses were all numbed, except
for her husband-lust. That was full-force.

Like someone who has a passion for trapping,
yet all his traps have fallen to pieces.
Like a rooster who crows at the wrong time,
a road that leads nowhere, a big fire
under an empty kettle.
                        She loves the racetrack,
but she has no horse, loves flute music
but has no flute, and no lips!

Even the most frantic of merchants slows down
in retirement. A dog's teeth drop out in old age.
It no longer challenges people. It eats dung.

But look at these sixty-year-old dogs,
male and female both, with their appetites
getting sharper by the minute!

An old dog loses its hair,
but these wrap themselves in satin.
Their greed for sex and money
keeps multiplying like puppies!

Someone says, "May your life be long,"
to one of these old dogs, and they think
it's the best thing that could happen.

But for an unconscious one with a closed-up wisdom eye,
long life is a curse, not a benediction.

If he or she could see one hair-tip of his state,
he would say back, "Yes. And may your life
be like this one I'm in."
                    One day a dervish,
a healthy, robust man who loved bread, was presented
with a loaf in the basket he always carried,
and he blessed the man from Gilan who gave it to him,
"God bring you back happy to your house."
                    The man re-
plied, "If it's the same empty house I recently left,
may God bring you back there, fellow."

Some people have a knack for humiliating
any speaker. They take any kind remark
and turn it sour.
                    But let's turn this topic in,
for whatever it might be worth, to the pawnshop
of the imagination, and return to the old woman.

Anyone advanced in years and not an Adept of the Way
should be called a *berouged old lady!*

He or she can neither give nor receive
spiritual delight. Neither has reality,
nor can absorb reality.
                    Such people have no beauty,
and no humility, but layer under layer
of the same rottenness,
like an onion that's gone bad.

They have no path,
no strong love,
and no surrendering sigh.

(*Mathnawi,* VI, 1222-1249)

Ayaz and the King's Pearl

One day the King assembled his courtiers.
He handed the Minister a glowing pearl.
"What would you say this is worth?"
                                    "More gold
than a hundred donkeys could carry."
                                    "Break it!"
"Sir, how could I waste your resources
like that?" The King presented him
with a robe of honor for his answer
and took back the pearl. He talked awhile
to the assembly on various topics.
                    Then he put the pearl
in the Chamberlain's hand. "What would it sell for?"
"Half a kingdom, God preserve it!"
                                    "Break it!"
"My hand could not move to do such a thing."
The King rewarded him with a robe of honor
and an increase in his salary, and so it went
with each of the fifty or sixty courtiers.

One by one, they imitated the Minister
and the Chamberlain and received new wealth.

Then the pearl was given to Ayaz.

"Can you say how splendid this is?"
"It's more than I can say."
                    "Then break it,
this second, into tiny pieces."
                    Ayaz had had a dream
about this, and he'd hidden two stones in his sleeve.
He crushed the pearl to powder between them.

As Joseph at the bottom of the well listened
to the end of his story, so such listeners
understand success and un-success as one thing.

Don't worry about forms.
If someone wants your horse,
let him have it. Horses are for
hurrying ahead of the others.

The court assembly screamed at the recklessness
of Ayaz, "How could you do that?"

"What the King says is worth more than any pearl,
I honor the King, not some colored stone."

The princes immediately fell on their knees
and put their foreheads on the ground.

Their sighs went up like a smoke-cloud
asking forgiveness. The King gestured
to his executioner as though to say,
"Take out this trash."
                              Ayaz sprang forward.
"Your mercy makes them bow like this.
Give them their lives! Let them keep hoping
for Union with you. They see their forgetfulness
now, as the drunken man did when he said,
'I didn't know what I was doing,' and then
someone pointed out, 'But you invited
that forgetfulness into you. You drank it.
There was a choice!'

They know deeply now how imitation
lulled them to sleep. Don't separate Yourself
from them. Look at all their heads against the floor.

Raise their faces into Yours. Let them wash
in your cool washing-place."

Ayaz and his speech always get to this point
and then the pen breaks. How can a saucer
contain the Ocean? The drunks break their cups,
but You poured that Wine!
                    Ayaz said, "You picked me
to crush the pearl. Don't punish the others
for my drunken obedience!
Punish them when I'm sober,
because I'll never be sober again.

Whoever bows down like they are bowing down
will not rise up in his old self again.

Like a gnat in Your Buttermilk,
they've become Your Buttermilk.

The mountains are trembling. Their map and compass
are the lines in Your Palm."
                    Husam,
I need a hundred mouths to say this,
but I only have this one!

A hundred thousand impressions from the Spirit
are wanting to come through here.
                         I feel stunned
in this abundance, crushed and dead.

(*Mathnawi,* V, 4035-4064, 4075-4079, 4083-4117, 4189-
4192, 4195-4215)

A Man and a Woman Arguing

One night in the desert
a poor Bedouin woman has this to say
to her husband,
                    "Everyone is happy
and prosperous, except us! We have no bread.
We have no spices. We have no water jug.
We barely have any clothes. No blankets
for the night. We fantasize that the full moon
is a cake. We reach for it! We're an embarrassment
even to the beggars. Everyone avoids us.

Arab men are supposed to be generous warriors,
but look at you, stumbling around! If some guest
were to come to us, we'd steal his rags
when he fell asleep. Who is your Guide
that leads you to this? We can't even get
a handful of lentils! Ten years' worth
of nothing, that's what we are!"
                                    She went on and on
like this. "If God is abundant, we must be following
an imposter. Who's leading us? Some fake,
that always says, *Tomorrow, illumination*
will bring you treasure, tomorrow.

As everyone knows, that never comes.
Though I guess, it happens very rarely, sometimes,
that a disciple following an imposter can somehow
surpass the pretender. But still I want to know
what this deprivation says about us."

The husband replied, finally,
                                "How long will you complain
about money and our prospects for money? The torrent
of our life has mostly gone by. Don't worry about

72

transient things. Think how the animals live.

The dove on the branch giving thanks.
The glorious singing of the nightingale.
The gnat. The elephant. Every living thing
trusts in God for its nourishment.

These pains that you feel are Messengers.
Listen to them. Turn them to sweetness. The night
is almost over. You were young once, and content.
Now you think about money all the time.

You used to *be* that money. You were a healthy vine.
Now you're a rotten fruit. You ought to be growing
sweeter and sweeter, but you've gone bad.

As my wife, you should be equal to me.
Like a pair of boots, if one is too tight,
the pair is of no use.

Like two folding doors, we can't be mismatched.
A lion does not mate with a wolf."

So this man who was happily poor
scolded his wife until daybreak,
when she responded,
                    "Don't talk to me
about your high station! Look how you act!
Spiritual arrogance is the ugliest of all things.
It's like a day that's cold and snowy,
and your clothes are wet too!

It's too much to bear!
And don't call me your mate, you fraud!
You scramble after scraps of bone
with the dogs.

You're not as satisfied as you pretend!
You're the snake and the snake-charmer
at the same time, but you don't know it.
You're charming a snake for money,
and the snake is charming you.

You talk about God a lot, and you make me feel guilty
by using that word. You better watch out!
That Word will poison you, if you use it
to have power over me."

So the rough volume of her talking
fell on the husband, and he fought back,

                                         "Woman,
this poverty is my deepest joy.
This bare way of life is honest and beautiful.
We can hide nothing when we're like this.
You say I'm really arrogant and greedy,
and you say I'm a snake-charmer and a snake,
but those nicknames are for you.

In your anger and your wantings
you see those qualities in me.
I want nothing from this world.

You're like a child that has turned round and round,
and now you think the house is turning.

It's your eyes that see wrong. Be patient,
and you'll see the blessings and the Lord's Light
in how we live."
                    This argument continued
throughout the day, and even longer.

(*Mathnawi*, I, 2252-2364, 2372-2374)

Muhammed and the Huge Eater

Husam demands that we begin Book V.
Ziya-Haqq, the Radiance of Truth,

                         Husamuddin,

Master to the Pure Masters,
if my human throat were not so narrow,
I would praise you as you should be praised,
in some language other than this word-language,
but a domestic fowl is not a falcon.
We must mix the varnish we have
and brush it on.

I'm not talking to materialists. When I mention Husam,
I speak only to those who know spiritual secrets.
Praise is simply drawing back the curtains
to let his qualities in.

                       The Sun,

of course, remains apart
from what I say.

What the sayer of Praise is really praising is
himself, by saying implicitly,
"My eyes are clear."

Likewise, someone who criticizes is criticizing
himself, saying implicitly, "I can't see very well
with my eyes so inflamed."

Don't ever feel sorry for someone
who wants to be the Sun, that other Sun,
the One that makes rotten things fresh.

And don't ever envy someone

who wants to be this world.

Husam is the Sun I mean.
He can't be understood with the mind, or said,
but we'll stumble and stagger trying to.
Just because you can't drink all that falls
doesn't mean you give up taking sips
of rainwater. If the nut
of the mystery can't be held,
at least let me touch the shell.

Husam, refresh my words, your words.
My words are only a husk to your knowing,
an earth-atmosphere to your enormous spaces.

What I say is meant only to point to that, to You,
so that whoever ever hears these words will not grieve
that they never had a chance to look.

Your Presence draws me out from vanity
and imagination and opinion.

Awe is the salve
that will heal our eyes.

And keen, constant listening.
Stay out in the open like a date palm
lifting its arms. Don't bore mouse-holes
in the ground, arguing inside some
doctrinal labyrinth.

That intellectual warp and woof keeps you wrapped
in blindness. And four other characteristics
keep you from loving. The *Qur'an* calls them
four birds. Say *Bismillah,* and chop the heads
off those mischief-birds.

The rooster of lust, the peacock of wanting
to be famous, the crow of ownership, and the duck
of urgency, kill them and revive them
in another form, changed and harmless.

There is a duck inside you.
Her bill is never still, searching through dry
and wet alike, like the robber in an empty house
cramming objects in his sack, pearls, chickpeas,
anything. Always thinking, "There's no time!
I won't get another chance!"

A True Person is more calm and deliberate.
He or she doesn't worry about interruptions.

But that duck is so afraid of missing out
that it's lost all generosity, and frighteningly expanded
its capacity to take in food.

A large group of unbelievers
once came to see Muhammed,
knowing he would feed them.

Muhammed told his Friends,
"Divide these guests among you and tend to them.
Since you are all filled with me,
it will be as though I am the host."

Each Friend of Muhammed chose a guest,
but there was one huge person left behind.
He sat in the entrance of the mosque
like thick dregs in a cup.

So Muhammed invited the man to his own household,
where the enormous son of a Ghuzz Turk ate everything,

the milk of seven goats and enough food
for eighteen people!

The others in the house were furious.
When the man went to bed, the maid slammed the door
behind him and chained it shut, out of meanness
and resentment. Around midnight, the man
felt several strong urges at once.

But the door! He works it,
puts a blade through the crack. Nothing.
The urgency increases. The room contracts.
He falls back into a confused sleep and dreams
of a desolate place, since he himself is
such a desolate place.

So, dreaming he's by himself,
he squeezes out a huge amount,
and another huge amount.

But he soon becomes conscious enough
to know that the covers he gathers around him
are full of shit. He shakes with spasms of the shame
that usually keeps men from doing such things.

He thinks, "My sleep is worse than my being awake.
The waking is just full of food.
My sleep is all *this*."

Now he's crying, bitterly embarrassed,
waiting for dawn and the noise of the door opening,
hoping that somehow he can get out
without anyone seeing him as he is.

I'll shorten it. The door opens. He's saved.
Muhammed comes at dawn. He opens the door

78

and becomes invisible so the man won't feel ashamed,
so he can escape and wash himself
and not have to face the door-opener.

Someone completely absorbed in Allah like Muhammed
can do this. Muhammed had seen all that went on
in the night, but He held back from letting the man out,
until all happened as it needed to happen.

Many actions which seem cruel
are from a deep Friendship.
Many demolitions are actually renovations.

Later, a meddlesome servant
brought Muhammed the bedclothes.
"Look what your guest has done!"

Muhammed smiles, himself a mercy given to all beings,
"Bring me a bucket of water."

Everyone jumps up, "No! Let us do this.
We live to serve you, and this is the kind of hand-work
we can do. Yours is the inner heart-work."

"I know that, but this is an extraordinary occasion."

A Voice inside him is saying, "There is great wisdom
in washing these bedclothes. Wash them."

Meanwhile, the man who soiled the covers and fled
is returning to Muhammed's house. He has left behind
an amulet that he always carried.

He enters and sees the Hands of God
washing his incredibly dirty linen.

He forgets the amulet. A great love suddenly enters him.
He tears his shirt open. He strikes his head
against the wall and the door. Blood
pours from his nose.

People come from other parts of the house.
He's shrieking, "Stay away!"
He hits his head, "I have no understanding!"
He prostrates himself before Muhammed.
"You are the Whole. I am a despicable, tiny,
meaningless piece. I can't look at You."
He's quiet and quivering with remorse.

Muhammed bends over and holds him and caresses him
and opens his inner knowing.

The cloud weeps, and then the garden sprouts.
The baby cries, and the mother's milk flows.
The Nurse of Creation has said, *Let them cry a lot.*

This rain-weeping and sun-burning twine together
to make us grow. Keep your intelligence white-hot
and your grief glistening, so your life will stay fresh.
Cry easily like a little child.

Let body-needs dwindle and soul-decisions increase.
Diminish what you give your physical self.
Your spiritual eye will begin to open.

When the body empties and stays empty,
God fills it with musk and mother-of-pearl.
That way a man gives his dung and gets purity.

Listen to the Prophets, not to some adolescent boy.
The foundation and the walls of the spiritual life
are made of self-denials and disciplines.

Stay with Friends who support you in these.
Talk with them about sacred texts,
and how you're doing, and how they're doing,
and keep your practices together.

(*Mathnawi,* V, 1-149, 163, 167)

The Pear Tree

To the Prophet, everything is soaked in Glory.
To us, things look inert. To Him,
the hill is in motion like the stream.
He hears a subtle conversation between
the clod and the brick. We don't.

There is no difference in awareness more extreme
than between His and ours. We see all graves the same,
whereas He sees one a garden, and one an ugly pit.

The sensual say, "Why is the Prophet so solemn?
What does He have against pleasure?" The saints reply,
"Come into our eyes, so you can hear
the laughter opening out."

You're seeing things reversed
as from the top of a pear tree,
the pear tree of phenomena.

All you see from there is a thorn thicket
full of scorpions. When you climb down,
you'll see a crowd of rosy children
with their nurses.

Once there was a woman
who wanted to make love with her lover
in the presence of her gullible husband.
She says to him,
                     "Lucky you, I'm going to climb
the tree and gather some fruit."
                                   In the top of the tree
she starts screaming and pointing at her husband,

"Who is that woman you're lying on top of?"
"You've lost your mind," says the husband.
"I'm standing here by myself."
                    "I see what you're doing,
you humping bastard!"
                    "Come down," he says,
"You're getting senile. I'll pick the fruit."

She climbs down, and he climbs up. Immediately
she and her lover begin what they enjoy.
"Hey whore, what's going on?"
                    "Don't be silly,"
she says from underneath. "I'm here by myself.
It must be the tree making the illusion.
When I was up there, I saw things just as weird.
Climb down, so you can see right."

Joking is teaching. Don't be fooled by the lightness,
or the vulgarity. Jokes are serious.

Come down from the pear tree
that's been making you dizzy.
Pear tree of ego and jealousy.

The pear tree itself will change
because of your humility in climbing down.
True seeing is not easy.

Muhammed himself prayed for it,
"Show me each part from above and below
as You see it."

Now climb the pear tree again. Pear Tree of Being.
Pear tree and burning bush in one, the green fire
along its branches saying, This. *This*.

In the shade of this fiery tree
there's peace for your wantings.

What you are supposed to become,
what you should know, is in your climbing
up and down that tree,

with its roots in the damp ground
and its limbs in airiness.

(*Mathnawi,*VI, 3522-3574)

Two Ways of Coming Down a Mountain

One day a mule and a camel were put in the same stall.
"Why is it ...," began the mule,
"I've always wanted to know. Why do *I*
come stumbling down the mountain frightened,
with my pack saddle crooked, and the driver beating me,
while *you* glide down like pure felicity?
Have you been given some special dispensation?
Why don't you ever fall on your face like me?"

The camel: "Every smooth descent is a gift.
But also, there are differences between us.
Unlike yours, my head stays lifted high,
so that from the top, and all the way down,
I can see the foot of the mountain
and every hollow and rise, fold on fold.

A True Human Being does this in his life.
He can see even to his death-day, and he knows
what will happen from now until twenty years from now,
not only for himself but for everyone.
Intelligent Light lives in the vision
and the loving of such a saint.
                              Why?
                                        Because
that's where it feels most at home.
Joseph dreamed that the sun and the moon
bowed down to worship him. Ten years went by,
and that came to be. The saying, 'He sees
by God's Light,' is not an idle idiom.
It means something.
                        There is a Light that can split
this earth-and-sky light to smithereens. That Light

is not seen with your eye. Your animal eye sees
only the next step, what's directly in front of you.

Another difference between us
is that my eye is clearer,
and my nature purer."

The mule responded, "You're right. Everything you say
is the truth."
                    He began to cry. He knelt
at the camel's feet. "Can I serve you in some way?
Will you let me serve you?"

"Since you've made this confession in my presence,
you will be spared the contaminations of Time.
Your stumbling disposition was not your deepest self.
Like Adam's, your lapse was temporary.

Your crying has taken you
inside the text that says,

                    Come in among My workers,

and the one that says,

                    Enter into Paradise.

You have found a secret way in.
You were fire, and now Light.
You were an unripe grape.
Now ripe, and now a raisin.

You were a tiny star-point.
Now the Sun. Live the deep joy
of knowing this."
                    Oh Husam, pour honey

in this milk. Stir it, so it won't turn sour.
Combine this with the Ocean of What We Were
Before Creation.
                    Roar the Lion-Knowledge.
Write this with gold Ocean-Ink,
so that whoever reads it
can grow in the Spirit.

(*Mathnawi*, IV, 3377-3382, 3389-3404, 3407-3430)

Spilling the Rose Oil

There was a grocer with a fine parrot,
which could talk intelligently to customers
in several languages and to the merchants
bringing fruits and vegetables.
                              He could also sing
sweet songs in his parrot language. He sat all day
on the back of the grocer's bench and held forth
generously.
            Once when the grocer was gone for a moment,
the parrot accidentally knocked over some bottles
of rose oil from a shelf above the bench.
                              The grocer
came back and sat down with great confidence
and high good-humor as a merchant always does
in front of his shop.
                      Then he realized that his clothes
were soaked in greasy rose oil. He bopped the parrot
on the head so that the top feathers came out
and the parrot looked bald.
                            For several days afterward
the parrot was quiet. It said nothing
in any language, not even its own.
                                  The grocer felt
terrible. Three days and three nights he grieved
and repented that he had silenced his Friend.

He felt his well-being and his prosperity leaving him.
He gave gifts to every dervish that he saw,
hoping to restore the speech of the parrot.

Finally a bareheaded dervish came by
with a head as bald as a begging bowl.

Hey-hey,
screeched the parrot, *Here's another klutz*
who spilt some rose oil!
                              Don't judge the Holy Ones
by yourself. The word "lion" sounds like "lying,"
but the inner qualities are so dissimilar!

People have wandered from the true way
because they can't recognize the Helpers
for what they are.

All human beings are not the same.
Some hymenoptera make poison for their stingers.
Others make honey. Some deer just make dung,
while others make musk from the same grass.

Two reeds in the water: One's hollow. The other,
full of sugarcane. One person eats and generates
greed and anger. Another, nothing but Love.

Bitter water and sweet water
both look clear. It takes someone
who can taste
                    to know the difference
                                    between which is sweet
and of the Spirit, and which is not,
                          a difference as wide
as a seventy-year journey!

(*Mathnawi*, I, 247-277)

When a Madman Smiles at You

Galen, the great physician, asked one of his assistants
to give him a certain medicine.
                              "Master, that medicine
is for crazy people! You're far from needing that!"

Galen: "Yesterday a madman turned and smiled at me,
did his eyebrows up and down, and touched my sleeve.
He wouldn't have done that if he hadn't recognized
in me someone congenial."
                              Anyone that feels drawn,
for however short a time, to anyone else,
those two share a common consciousness.

It's only in the grave that unlike beings associate.
A wise man once remarked, "I saw a crow and a stork
flying together, and I couldn't understand it,
until I investigated and found what they shared.
They were both lame."
                              There's a reason why the beetle
leaves the rose garden. He can't stand
all that loveliness.
                              He wants to live in rotten dung,
not with nightingales and flowers.
                              Watch who avoids you.
That too, reveals your inner qualities.

The mark of eternity in Adam was not only
that the angels bowed to him,
                              but that Satan wouldn't.

(*Mathnawi*, II, 2095-2105, 2112-2123)

90

A Song About a Donkey

The following is about the dangers
of imitating others in your spiritual life.

Meet the Friend on your own.
Try to dissolve out of selfishness
into a Voice beyond those limits.

A wandering Sufi came with his donkey
to a community of Sufis who were very poor.
He fed the donkey and gave it water,
left it with his servant, and went inside.

Immediately, a group of the resident Sufis
sold the donkey and bought food and candles
for a feast.
           There was jubilation in the monastery!
No more patience and three-day fasting!

If you are rich and full-fed, don't laugh
at the impulsiveness of the poor.
They were not acting from their souls,
but they were acting out of some necessity.

The traveler joined in the festivities.
They paid constant attention to him,
caressing him, honoring him.
                The sema began.
There was smoke from the kitchen,
dust from the feet hitting the floor,
and ecstasy from the longing of the dancers.

Their hands were waving.

Their foreheads swept low across the dais.
It had been a long wait for such an occasion.

Sufis always have to wait a long time
for their desire. That's why they're such
great eaters!
        The Sufi who feeds on Light, though,
is different, but there's only one of those
in a thousand. The rest live under
that one's protection.
        The sema ran its course
and ended. The poet began to sing a deep grief-song,
"The donkey is gone, my son. Your donkey is gone."

Everyone joined in, clapping their hands and singing
over and over, "The donkey is gone, my son.
Your donkey is gone."
        And the visiting Sufi
sang more passionately than all the rest. Finally,
it was dawn, and they parted with many goodbyes.
The banquet room was empty. The man brought out
his baggage and called to his servant,
"Where's my donkey?"
        "Look at you!"
        "What do you mean?"
"They sold your donkey! That's how we had
such a celebration!"
        "Why didn't you come and tell me?"
"Several times I came near, but you were always
singing so loudly, 'The donkey's gone,
the donkey's gone,' that I thought you knew.
I thought you had a secret insight"
        "Yes.
It was my imitation of their joy that caused this."

Even the good delight of friends is at first

a reflection in you. Stay with them
until it becomes a realization.
                              The imitation here
came from the man's desire to be honored.
It deafened him to what was being
so constantly said.

Remember there's only one reason
to do anything: A meeting with the Friend
is the only real payment.

(*Mathnawi*, II, 512-576)

Childhood Friends

You may have heard, it's the custom for Kings
to let warriors stand on the left, the side of the heart,
and courage. On the right, they put the Chancellor,
and various secretaries, because the practice
of bookkeeping and writing usually belongs
to the right hand. In the center,
                              the Sufis,
because in meditation they become mirrors.
The King can look at their faces
and see his original state.

Give the beautiful ones mirrors,
and let them fall in love with themselves.

That way they polish their souls
and kindle remembering in others.

A close childhood friend once came to visit Joseph.
They had shared the secrets that children tell each other
when they're lying on their pillows at night
before they go to sleep. These two
were completely truthful
with each other.

The friend asked, "What was it like when you realized
your brothers were jealous and what they planned to do?"

"I felt like a lion with a chain around its neck.
Not degraded by the chain, and not complaining,
but just waiting for my power to be recognized."

"How about down in the well, and in prison?

94

How was it then?"
                    "Like the moon when it's getting
smaller, yet knowing the fullness to come.
Like a seed pearl ground in the mortar for medicine,
that knows it will now be the light in a human eye.

Like a wheat grain that breaks open in the ground,
then grows, then gets harvested, then crushed in the mill
for flour, then baked, then crushed again between teeth
to become a person's deepest understanding.
Lost in Love, like the songs the planters sing
the night after they sow the seed."
                              There is no end
to any of this.
              Back to something else the good man
and Joseph talked about.
                        "Ah my Friend, what have you
brought me? You know a traveler should not arrive
empty-handed at the door of a friend like me.
That's going to the grinding stone without your wheat.
God will ask at the Resurrection, 'Did you bring Me
a present? Did you forget? Did you think
you wouldn't see Me?'"
                      Joseph kept teasing,
"Let's have it. I want my gift!"

The guest began, "You can't imagine how I've looked
for something for you. Nothing seemed appropriate.
You don't take gold down into a goldmine,
or a drop of water to the Sea of Oman!
                              Everything
I thought of was like bringing cumin seed
to Kirmanshah where cumin comes from.

You have all seeds in your barn. You even have my love
and my soul, so I can't even bring those.

95

I've brought you a mirror. Look at yourself,
and remember me."
                              He took the mirror out from his robe
where he was hiding it.
                              What is the mirror of being?
Non-being. Always bring a mirror of non-existence
as a gift. Any other present is foolish.

Let the poor man look deep into generosity.
Let bread see a hungry man.
Let kindling behold a spark from the flint.

An empty mirror and your worst destructive habits,
when they are held up to each other,
that's when the real making begins.
That's what art and crafting are.

A tailor needs a torn garment to practice his expertise.
The trunks of trees must be cut and cut again
so they can be used for fine carpentry.

Your doctor must have a broken leg to doctor.
Your defects are the ways that glory gets manifested.
Whoever sees clearly what's diseased in himself
begins to gallop on the Way.

There is nothing worse
than thinking you are well enough.
More than anything, self-complacency
blocks the workmanship.

Put your vileness up to a mirror and weep.
Get that self-satisfaction flowing out of you!
Satan thought, "I am better than Adam,"
and that *better than* is still strongly in us.

Your stream-water may look clean,
but there's unstirred matter on the bottom.
Your Sheikh can dig a side-channel
that will drain that waste off.

Trust your wound to a Teacher's surgery.
Flies collect on a wound. They cover it,
those flies of your self-protecting feelings,
your love for what you think is yours.

Let a Teacher wave away the flies
and put a plaster on the wound.

Don't turn your head. Keep looking
at the bandaged place. That's where
the Light enters you.
                    And don't believe for a moment
that you're healing yourself.

(*Mathnawi*, I, 3150-3175, 3192-3227)

Chinese Art and Greek Art

The Prophet said, "There are some who see Me
by the same Light in which I am seeing them.
Our natures are ONE.
                    Without reference to any strands
of lineage, without reference to texts or traditions,
we drink the Life-Water together."
                                Here's a story
about that hidden mystery:
                    The Chinese and the Greeks
were arguing as to who were the better artists.
The King said,
                "We'll settle this matter with a debate."
The Chinese began talking,
but the Greeks wouldn't say anything.
They left.
                The Chinese suggested then
that they each be given a room to work on
with their artistry, two rooms facing each other
and divided by a curtain.
                    The Chinese asked the King
for a hundred colors, all the variations,
and each morning they came to where
the dyes were kept and took them all.
The Greeks took no colors.
"They're not part of our work."
                            They went to their room
and began cleaning and polishing the walls. All day
every day they made those walls as pure and clear
as an open sky.
                    There is a way that leads from all-colors
to colorlessness. Know that the magnificent variety
of the clouds and the weather comes from

the total simplicity of the sun and the moon.

The Chinese finished, and they were so happy.
They beat the drums in the joy of completion.

The King entered their room,
astonished by the gorgeous color and detail.

The Greeks then pulled the curtain dividing the rooms.
The Chinese figures and images shimmeringly reflected
on the clear Greek walls. They lived there,
even more beautifully, and always
changing in the light.

The Greek art is the Sufi way.
They don't study books of philosophical thought.

They make their loving clearer and clearer.
No wantings, no anger. In that purity
they receive and reflect the images of every moment,
from here, from the stars, from the void.

They take them in
as though they were seeing
with the Lighted Clarity
that sees them.

(*Mathnawi,* I, 3462-3485, 3499)

Tattooing in Qazwin

In Qazwin, they have a custom of tattooing themselves
for good luck, with a blue ink, on the back
of the hand, the shoulder, wherever.

A certain man there goes to his barber
and asks to be given a powerful, heroic, Blue Lion
on his shoulder blade. "And do it with flair!
I've got Leo Ascending. I want plenty of blue!"

But as soon as the needle starts pricking,
he howls,
        "What are you doing?"
                      "The lion."
"Which limb did you start with?"
                      "I began with the tail."
"Well, leave out the tail. That lion's rump
is in a bad place for me. It cuts off my wind."

The barber continues, and immediately
the man yells out,
        "Oooooooo! Which part now?"
                      "The ear."
"Doc, let's do a lion with no ears this time."
                      The barber
shakes his head, and once more the needle,
and once more the wailing,
        "Where are you now?"
                      "The belly."
"I like a lion without a belly."
                      The Master Lion-Maker
stands for a long time with his fingers in his teeth.
Finally, he throws the needle down.

100

"No one has ever been asked
to do such a thing! To create a lion
without a tail or a head or a stomach.
God himself could not do it!"

Brother, stand the pain.
Escape the poison of your impulses.
The sky will bow to your beauty, if you do.
Learn to light the candle. Rise with the sun.
Turn away from the cave of your sleeping.
That way a thorn expands to a Rose.
A particular glows with the Universal.

What is it to praise?
Make yourself particles.

What is it to know something of God?
Burn inside that Presence. Burn up.

Copper melts in the healing elixir.
So melt your self in the Mixture
that Sustains Existence.

You tighten your two hands together,
determined not to give up saying "I" and "we."
This tightening blocks you.

(*Mathnawi*, I, 2981-3021)

A Subtle Theological Point

There was a popular preacher,
very subtle in his exegesis. A huge crowd
always gathered when he spoke.

Juhi wanted to hear, so he put on a long mantle,
a woman's chadar, and went in the mosque
on the less-crowded women's side, undetected.

Someone handed a note discreetly to the preacher
asking whether hair in the private regions
causes difficulty in ritual prayers.

The preacher replied openly,
        "If your hair is long
in the pubic region, then you are not properly prepared
for prayer. You may wish to use a depilatory, or a razor,
to remove those long hairs."
        The questioner continued,
"But to what length should they be cut
to make my praying right?"
        The preacher, "As long as
the length does not exceed the width of a grain of barley,
your hair-cutting will be religiously perfect,
O Asker of Many Questions!"
        At once Juhi whispered
to the woman beside him, "Sister, see if the hair
in my pubic region is as it should be, pleasing
to God. Feel with your hand whether it's right."

The woman put her hand between his legs
and touched his penis. She screamed out.

102

The preacher said, "My discourse
must have touched her heart."

                    "It's not so much,"
replied Juhi, "her heart that's impressed
as her hand, but O if a wise man
like you could so touch
a heart!"

Reader,
when Divine Love reached and brushed
only just so lightly
Pharaoh's magicians, they no longer
knew a hand from a staff!

If you take away a walkingstick
from an old man, he will be more grieved
than those Egyptian shamans were
when they had their hands and feet amputated!

Their cry was, "No harm. This is no harm
to us! We are no longer in these bodies.
We live within God."

                    Blessed is anyone
who knows who he or she really is
and builds a place to live there.

A child loves walnuts and raisins more than anything.
A mature spirit sees those delights for what they are.

To your deepest being the body
is like a raisin-and-walnut snack.
Your soul has no doubts about
what's more real.

Every man has testicles and hair,
as every male goat has a beard and balls.

One goat, though, leads the group to the butcher.
He combs his beard and says,
"I'm in charge here."

Yes, in charge of death and worrying!

Forget your beard and your self-importance.
Be an invisible guide, like the scent of roses
that shows where the inner garden is.

(*Mathnawi,* V, 3325-3350)

A One-Grain Ant

An ant trembles along
with its one grain of wheat,
afraid it might lose that, not knowing
how wide and covered with grain the threshing-floor is.

Likewise, you are so devoted to your wheat-grain body.
That's not all you are! There's much more.
Look around with your other Eye.

Look at Saturn. Look at Solomon!
Whatever a human being truly sees,
he or she becomes. That's the nature
of this existence.
                    When a jar opens into the Ocean,
it can drown a mountain range. Muhammed opened
his language, and you know what came through!

One way of seeing sees only a road.
Another sees a home. It's always Home.

The former is dualistic, gauging who's ahead
and who's behind. The latter sees everything
at once, and reversed, so that being last
is winning, and dying is living,
as well as dying.

You have to experience this Truth
to know what it is.

(*Mathnawi*,VI, 806-821)

The Private Banquet

Muhammed, in the Presence of Gabriel,
$\qquad\qquad\qquad\qquad$"Friend,
let me see You as you really are. Let me look
as an interested observer looks at his Interest.

"You could not endure it. The sense of sight
is too weak to take in this Reality."

"But show Yourself anyway, that I can understand
what may not be known with the senses."

The body-senses are wavering and blurry,
but there is a clear fire inside,
$\qquad\qquad\qquad\qquad$a flame like Abraham,
that is Alpha and Omega.
$\qquad\qquad\qquad\qquad\qquad$Man seems to be derived,
evolved, from this planet, but Essentially,
Man is the Origin of the world. Remember this!

A tiny gnat's outward form flies around and around
in pain and wanting, while the gnat's inward nature
includes the entire galactic whirling of the Universe!

Muhammed persisted in his request,
and Gabriel revealed a single feather
that reached from the East to the West,
a glimpse that would have instantly crumbled to powder
a mountain range.
$\qquad\qquad\qquad\qquad$Muhammed stared, senseless.
Gabriel came and held him in his arms.
$\qquad\qquad\qquad\qquad\qquad\qquad$Awe serves
for strangers. This close-hugging love

106

is for Friends.
          Kings have formidable guards around them
with swords drawn, a public show of power
that keeps order and reduces arrogance and mischief
and other disasters.
                    But when the King comes
to the private banquet with His Friends,
there's harp music and the flute.
No kettle drums.
                    And no keeping accounts,
no judging behavior, no helmets, no armor.

Just silk and music and beautiful women bringing cups.
You know how it is, but who can say it!

Conclude this part, my Friend,
and lead us the way we should go.

(*Mathnawi,* IV, 3755-3785)

107

Cry Out in Your Weakness

A dragon was pulling a bear into its terrible mouth.

A courageous man went and rescued the bear.
There are such helpers in the world, who rush to save
anyone who cries out. Like Mercy itself,
they run toward the screaming.

And they can't be bought off.
If you were to ask one of those, "Why did you come
so quickly?" He or she would say, "Because I heard
your helplessness."
                   Where lowland is,
that's where water goes. All medicine wants
is pain to cure.
                        And don't just ask for one mercy.
Let them flood in. Let the sky open under your feet.
Take the cotton out of your ears, the cotton
of consolations, so you can hear the sphere-music.

Push the hair out of your eyes.
Blow the phlegm from your nose,
and from your brain.

Let the Wind breeze through.
Leave no residue in yourself from that bilious fever.
Take the cure for impotence,
that your manhood may shoot forth,
and a hundred new beings come of your coming.

Tear the binding from around the foot
of your soul, and let it race around the track
in front of the crowd. Loosen the knot of greed

108

so tight on your neck. Accept your new good luck.

Give your weakness
to One Who Helps.

Crying out loud and weeping are great resources.
A nursing mother, all she does
is wait to hear her child.

Just a little beginning-whimper,
and she's there.

God created the child, that is, your wanting,
so that it might cry out, so that milk might come.

Cry out! Don't be stolid and silent
with your pain. Lament! And let the milk
of Loving flow into you.

The hard rain and wind
are ways the cloud has
to take care of us.

Be patient.
Respond to every call
that excites your spirit.

Ignore those that make you fearful
and sad, that degrade you
back toward disease and death.

(*Mathnawi,* II, 1932-1960)

Flowing Gifts

It takes too long to tell the whole story
of these stories!
                        Back to the debtor who was praying
at this Master's grave, and the court bailiff
who heard him, who also loved the Master,
and who then took him home and gave him
a hundred dinars and fed him roast meat
and told him stories,
                        so that roses began to open
in the debtor's chest, the way it happens when prosperity
comes after a long time of not having much.

Midnight, and they were still up talking.
Then sleep took them to the meadow
where the Spirit feeds.

And that night the bailiff dreamed that he saw the Master.
"My excellent bailiff, I see what you've done, and I hear
how you're talking. But in the Spirit we must
keep silent. The Unseen cannot be told.
                        Otherwise,
your mortality-meat would not get cooked as it should.
You would stay half-raw. Here in the Spirit we can see
the final results of what we did in the material world.
What comes of our generosities is especially beautiful.

Now listen to the gifts I have for our new Friend,
the man who owes so much money.

I knew he would come to be here with you,
so I packed some jewels away for him.
He owes nine thousand gold pieces.

110

These are more than enough for that.

They're in a jar with his name on it buried in a vault.
I'll show you where. Before I died, I wrote this down
in a little notebook, and I meant to give it to him,
but Death took me. There are rubies and pearls
and topazes, a great fortune!
                              If he says he doesn't need
that much, let him give it to whoever he wants to.

Milk never returns to the breast.
It keeps flowing out. Muhammed said
that anybody who takes a gift back
is like a dog licking its vomit.

Two years ago I hid this wealth,
and it is only for him to dispense.
It must go through him
to those it's supposed to reach."

The Master told two other mysteries to the bailiff,
but I cannot reveal those. Some secrets must be kept,
and besides, this *Mathnawi* has to stay within
some limits!

The bailiff woke, happier than he'd ever been, snapping
his fingers, singing love songs, and then sad songs,
all kinds of songs. The debtor, his guest, said,

"What did you dream of that you woke so drunken?
You woke without any boundaries!
The city can't hold you, nor can the desert!
Not even your circle of Friends
can hold you today. You're free!"

"... I saw the Master ...

111

I saw the Giver..."
                    The bailiff rambled on,
singing and talking. He lay down on his back,
laughing and babbling, in the middle of his room.

With a crowd of people around him
he told the debtor everything.

(*Mathnawi,*VI, 3518-3565)

A Goat Kneels!

The inner being of a human being
is a jungle. Sometimes wolves dominate,
sometimes wild hogs. Be wary when you breathe!

At one moment gentle, generous qualities,
like Joseph's, pass from one nature to another.
The next moment vicious qualities
move in hidden ways.

Wisdom slips for a while into an ox!
A restless, recalcitrant horse suddenly
becomes obedient and smooth-gaited.

A bear begins to dance.
A goat kneels!

Human consciousness goes into a dog,
and that dog becomes a shepherd,
or a hunter.

In the Cave of the Seven Sleepers
even the dogs were seekers.

At every moment a new species rises in the chest—
now a demon, now an angel, now a wild animal.

There are also those in this amazing jungle
who can absorb you into their own surrender.

If you have to stalk and steal something,
steal from them!

(*Mathnawi*, II, 1416-1429)

Three Creatures

In the Sayings of Muhammed it's told
that there are three kinds of creatures:

One made entirely of clear reason
and generosity, always prostrated in worship.
That one is called the angel.

Another has no knowledge,
lives only to eat and sleep,
and never considers the future.
It's called the animal.

The third descends from Adam
and is called human,
half-angel, half-donkey.

Half of that one turns toward sensuality,
and half toward clarity.

All of these have human shapes,
but one is as pure as Gabriel,
one totally undisciplined and angry,
and the other wrestles between the two.

The animal kind of human is a most subtle craftsman.
He knows how to weave gold-embroidered robes,
how to find pearls on the ocean bottom,
and how to construct the elaborate artifices
of geometry and astronomy, philosophy and medicine.

Those arts and sciences are the roof and walls
of the stable where the animal lives protected

for a few days, though their practitioners
call them "mysteries."

The real Way opens only with Love.
When that waking comes, the animal-man
finally understands his dreams.

It's like he's been trying to read something
upside-down!
                    He turns it over,
and the meaning is instantly clear.

(*Mathnawi*, IV, 1497-1525)

115

The Ocean Duck

You're a wild Ocean-Duck
that has been raised with chickens!

Your true mother lived on the Ocean,
but your nurse was a domestic land-bird.

Your deepest soul-instincts are toward the Ocean.
Whatever land-moves you have
you learned from your nurse, the hen.
It's time now to join the ducks!

Your nurse will warn you about saltwater,
but don't listen! The Ocean's your home,
not that stinking henhouse.

You are a King, a son of Adam, who can tread water,
as well as the ground. Angels don't walk the earth,
and animals don't swim in the spiritual Ocean.

You're a man or a woman.
You do both. You stumble along, and you soar
in great circles through the sky.

We are waterbirds, my son.
The Ocean knows our language and hears us,
and replies. The sea is our Solomon.

Walk into that, and let the David-Water
make us lovely chain-mail with its ripples.

The Ocean is always around us, but sometimes
through vanity and forgetfulness we get seasick.

As thunder sometimes gives a thirsty man
a headache, when he forgets it's bringing rain.
He keeps hoping for something from the dry creek-bed.
Don't look to secondary causes!

Once an ascetic lived far out in the desert,
and pilgrims would come to marvel at him.

Enraptured, he stood on sand hot enough
to make water boil, yet in the desert wind
he was cool and moist
as though in a freshly watered garden.

His bare feet seemed wrapped in silk
and his body in a breeze.

The pilgrims waited. Finally he came back
from his absorbed state to be one of them,
very bright and alive.
                         Water was trickling
from his face and garments
as though from ablutions.
                         "Where did it come from?"
they asked. He pointed upward.
                         "But does it come
whenever you want it to? With no well and no rope!
Tell us more about this."
                         The ascetic prayed,
"Answer these pilgrims' questions, You Who
brought space into view from non-spatiality.
Let these pilgrims see where their sustaining
comes from."
                 In the middle of that a cloud appeared,
a big elephant of a cloud,
that began to spray down trunkfuls
of rainwater, flooding the ditches and hollows.

The pilgrims opened their waterskins
and let them be filled.

One group immediately cut the cords of doubt
and were freed.
                    Another group let their faith
begin to grow slowly.
                    And a third segment
of the pilgrims were sour and skeptical
before they came, and sour and skeptical
afterwards.
                    And that's the end of that story!

(*Mathnawi,* II, 3766-3810)

An Early Morning Eye

When you start some new work,
you give in completely to it.

You're excited,
because the Creator keeps you
from seeing what's missing.

Your heatedness hides that,
so you do the work, and then look back
and see the nature of it.

If you'd seen that at first,
you wouldn't have done anything!

Don't worry about repenting.
Do the work that's given,
and learn from it.

If you become addicted to looking back,
half your life will be spent in distraction,
and the other half in regret.

You can live better than that!
Find happier friends.

Say: Show me the faults
of my destructive actions, but don't show me
what's wrong with my good work.
That way I won't get disgusted and quit!

Solomon had a habit of visiting the mosque at dawn,
because then he could see

with an early morning eye
the new spirit-plants that were growing.

Encourage that freshness
in yourself, and not what clouds you
with dullness and futility.

(*Mathnawi,* IV, 1332-1342, 1353-1357)

Collect the Pieces

The gold of your intelligence
is scattered over many clippings and bits
of wanting. Bring them all together
in one place. How else can I stamp it?

Think how a great city concentrates
around a point. Damascus or Samarcand.
Grain by grain, collect the pieces.

The Beloved then becomes food and water,
lamp and helper, dessert and wine.
Many-ness is confusion and intellectual talk.

Silence gives answers. I know that,
but my mouth keeps opening involuntarily
like a yawn or a sneeze.

(*Mathnawi,* IV, 3287-3299)

Following the Sunset

Sheikh Maghribi, whose name means,
"The Place of Sunset," declares,
                              "For sixty years
I have never known the quality of night.
I have not seen darkness."

His companions say this is true.
"We follow him into the desert, through steep ditches
and thorns. He lights up the landscape
like a full moon.
                    He doesn't look behind,
but he calls to us, *Watch out for the ravine!*
Go left! Turn right! There are thorns through there!

At daylight, we kiss his bare feet,
as white and smooth as a bride's.
No trace of mud, no scratch,
or any bruise from the terrain."

God made sunset a sunrise.
This One's light protects
from scorpions and thieves.

The text says, "On the Day when the Prophet
is not put to shame," and the text means,
                              Light goes before,
tearing danger to pieces.
                    Light will increase
at the Resurrection, but we should beg to have it now,
in the clouds and mist of these bodies.

(*Mathnawi*, IV, 598-613)

Solomon and Sheba

Queen Sheba loads forty mules with gold bricks
as gifts for Solomon. When her envoy and his party
reach the wide plain leading to Solomon's palace,
they see that the top layer of the entire plain
is pure gold. They travel on gold
for forty days.
                What foolishness to take gold
to Solomon, when the dirt of his land
is gold! You who think to offer
your intelligence, reconsider. The mind
is less than road-dust.

The embarrassing commonness they bring
slows them down. They argue. They discuss
turning back, but they continue,
carrying out the orders of their Queen.

Solomon laughs when he sees them unloading
gold bars.
                "When have I asked you
for a sop for my soup? I don't want gifts
from you. I want you to be ready
for the gifts I give.

You worship a planet that creates gold.
Worship instead the One who creates the universe.
You worship the sun. The sun is only a cook.
Think of a solar eclipse. What if you get attacked
at midnight? Who will help you then?"

These astronomical matters fade.
Another intimacy happens,

a sun at midnight,
with no East, no night or day.

The clearest intelligences faint
with seeing the solar system flickering,
so tiny in that immense Lightness.

Drops fall into a vapor, and the vapor explodes
into a galaxy. Half a ray strikes a patch of darkness.
A new sun appears.
                    One slight, alchemical gesture,
and Saturnine qualities form inside
the planet Saturn.

The sensuous eye needs sunlight to see.
Use another Eye.
                    Vision is luminous.
Sight is igneous, and sun-fire light very dark.

(*Mathnawi,* IV, 563-597)

In Between Stories

Turn from the Ocean now
toward dry land.

When you're with children, talk about toys.
From playthings, little by little, they reach
into deeper wisdom and clarity. Gradually,
they loose interest in their toys.

They have a sense of wholeness in them already.
If they were completely demented,
they wouldn't play at all.
                          Did you hear that?
It's the man who was looking for treasure.
He wants me to finish his story.
                          You didn't hear him?
Then he must be inside me yelling, "Over here!
Come over here!"
                          Don't think of him as a seeker, though.
Whatever he's looking for, he is that himself.
How can a lover be anything but the Beloved?

Every second he's bowing into a mirror.
If he could see for just a second one molecule
of what's there without fantasizing about it,
he'd explode.
                          His imagination, and he himself,
would vanish, with all his knowledge, obliterated
into a new birth, a perfectly clear view,
a Voice that says, *I am God.*

That same Voice told the angels to bow to Adam,
because they were identical with Adam.

It's the Voice that first said,
There is no Reality but God.
There is only God.
Husam pulls me by the ear now,
"Wash your mouth! By trying to say these things,
you conceal them. Just finish telling the story
about the dervish who was looking for treasure.

Your listeners love difficulties, not Unity!
Talk about world-troubles.
Don't distribute water from the Fountain.
They don't want that.
In fact, they've loaded themselves
with dirt clods to clog up the Fountain.
They'd like to shut it off!"

We are listeners as well as speakers
of this Mystery, both of us,
but who else will join
this strange Companionship?

That's what Husam wants to know!

(*Mathnawi*, VI, 2252-2277)

The Worm's Waking

This is how a human being can change:

There's a worm addicted to eating
grape leaves.
                    Suddenly, he wakes up,
call it Grace, whatever, something
wakes him, and he's no longer
a worm.
                    He's the entire vineyard,
and the orchard too, the fruit, the trunks,
a growing wisdom and joy
that doesn't need
to devour.

(*Mathnawi*, IV, 2537-2539)

Put This Design in Your Carpet

Spiritual experience is a modest woman
who only looks lovingly at one man.

It's a great River where ducks
live happily, and crows drown.

The visible bowl of form contains food
that is both nourishing and a source of heartburn.

There is an Unseen Presence we honor
that gives the gifts.

You're Water. We're the millstone.
You're Wind. We're the dust blown up into shapes.
You're Spirit. We're the opening and closing
of our hands. You're the Clarity.
We're this language that tries to say it.
You're the Joy. We're all the different kinds of laughing.

Any movement or sound is a profession of faith,
as the millstone grinding is explaining how it believes
in the River! No metaphor can say this,
but I can't stop pointing
to the Beauty.

Every moment and place says,
"Put this design in Your Carpet!"

Like the shepherd in Book II,
who wanted to pick the lice off God's robe,
and stitch up God's shoes, I want to be
in such a passionate adoration

that my tent gets pitched against the sky!

Let the Beloved come
and sit like a guard-dog
in front of that tent.

When the Ocean surges,
don't let me just hear it.
Let it splash inside my chest!

(*Mathnawi*,V, 3292-3299, 3310-3324)

Lovers Want Each Other Completely Naked

Some comment on the text, *The Spiritual World
is speaking, if we could only hear it.*

Every particle is eloquently alive. That Hearing
makes the way we usually are seem like
so much dead grass thrown out for cattle.

Someone who has tasted the air inside the Rose,
do you think he'd go back
to drinking wine in the steambath?

Your true Home is the seventh stage of spiritual growth,
Illiyyin, reached through purification and peacefulness.

There, you are still in your body,
and yet a living Master
of the Essence.

A worm enjoys crawling through dung. Not you.
Sip the sweet cup. The other one makes you blind.

A lifeless cloth doll is given to young girls,
because they don't know the love-play of living men.

A wooden sword suits little boys
before they have strength in their shoulders.
Some people are happy enough
looking at the painted pictures of saints in churches.

But those who have felt a bright inner connection
are not interested.

This is how it is with a True Human Being:
He or she is made of two figures.

One is here explaining subtle points.
The other is whispering with God.

One listens to these words.
The Other One's ears receive the Creation-Word, BE!

One eye watches these forms moving about,
while the Other takes in the dazzle
inside the text that says,

> *That Eye does not look away.*

One set of feet stands even with the others
in the line of worshipers at the mosque.
The Other set ambles in the sky.

To be clearer: Part of a True Person
is inside Time, and part is beyond Time.

The Time-part dies. The Other
is the Good Friend of Forever.

For That One,
a forty-day fast is not necessary.
The cave of such seclusion
would begin to glow
like the sun lived in it.

Abstinence, disbelief, unfaithfulness,
these words do not apply.

A True Person is like the vertical stroke of the *alif*.
There's nothing else there, just a naked line of Being.

When dregs become pure, they rise to the top.
The soul, like Adam, was told,
"Get out of the Garden!" And for a time,

hung suspended, head down.

A wicker basket sank in the Ocean,
and saw itself full of seawater, and decided
it could live independently.

It left the Ocean
and not a drop stayed in it.
But the Ocean took it back.

For no reason, the Ocean took it back.
For God's sake, stay near the sea!

Walk the beach.
Your face is pale
with being so separate,
but it will get redder.
Paleness wants Union.

Be lean with wanting that.
Walk out where there's no shade.
The network of shadows is a filter
that you no longer need.

Lovers want each other completely naked.
Loaves of fresh bread and beautifully prepared food
are saved for those who fast.

To a green horsefly what difference does it make?
He lights on the trivet under the pot.
He lights in the soup.

I am sinking in the Ocean
of this subject!

(*Mathnawi,*V, 3591-3634)

A House With Only One Door

One day a Sufi came back to his house
in the late morning, which he had never
been known to do.   His wife was there
with the local shoemaker! The Sufi husband
banged on the door. He had had some intuition
of this infidelity.
            The house had only one door.
The wife and her lover were engaged in
that even smaller cubicle where their desire
had taken them. There was no way to escape.

The woman had done this many times. It had seemed
like nothing much to her, a lighthearted matter,
but this time, with no escape possible,
it was like the Angel of Death was knocking.

The husband thought, "I'll pretend to be ignorant,
to torture them a little, as a man with dropsy
gets slowly worse, though every moment he thinks
he's getting better, or as the hyena-hunters
fool the hyena by saying, 'Where's the hyena,'
when they know exactly where the hyena is."

So there they were with no closet, no cellar, no attic.
It was the broad, flat plain of Resurrection Day,
with no place to conceal what they had done.

She threw a robe of her own over the shoemaker,
and opened the door. A very clumsy disguise.

Obviously, there was a man under the chadar,

unexplainable, and conspicuous
as a camel on a staircase.

She said,"This lady has come to visit.
Actually, she's interested in arranging a marriage
between her son and our daughter, though, of course,
our daughter is at school today, and her son
is out of town, but still she wanted
to discuss the matter."
                    "Why would such a fine lady
make an alliance with a wretched Sufi family
like ours?"
               "I mentioned that to her.
She claims that she likes our modest circumstances,
and the chastity of our marriage. Yes.
She admires the purity of this family
more than any social status."

The Sufi's wife went on like this
with such excessive hypocrisy, perfecting
the trap with her own cunning.

I tell this story to show the ugliness
of not being able to feel shame.

Real Lovers are never
so impudent as this
with each other.

(*Mathnawi,* IV,158-162,172,175-214)

134

The Importance of Gourdcrafting

There was a maidservant
who had cleverly trained a donkey
to perform the services of a man.

From a gourd,
she had carved a flanged device
to fit on the donkey's penis, to keep him
from going too far into her.

She had fashioned it just to the point
of her pleasure, and she greatly enjoyed
the arrangement, as often as she could!

She thrived, but the donkey was getting
a little thin and tired-looking.

The mistress began to investigate. One day
she peeked through a crack in the door
and saw the animal's marvelous member
and the delight of the girl
stretched under the donkey.

She said nothing. Later, she knocked on the door
and called the maid out on an errand,
a long and complicated errand.
I won't go into details.

The servant knew what was happening, though.
"Ah, my mistress," she thought to herself,
"you should not send away the expert.

When you begin to work without full knowledge,

you risk your life. Your shame keeps you
from asking me about the gourd, but you must
have that to join with this donkey.
There's a trick you don't know!"

But the woman was too fascinated with her idea
to consider any danger. She led the donkey in
and closed the door, thinking, "With no one around
I can shout in my pleasure."
                      She was dizzy
with anticipation, her vagina glowing
and singing like a nightingale.

She arranged the chair under the donkey,
as she had seen the girl do. She raised her legs
and pulled him into her.
                   Her fire kindled more,
and the donkey politely pushed as she urged him to,
pushed through and into her intestines,
and without a word, she died.

The chair fell one way,
and she the other.

The room was smeared with blood.
                  Reader,
have you ever seen anyone martyred
for a donkey? Remember what the *Qur'an* says
about the torment of disgracing yourself.

Don't sacrifice your life to your animal-soul!

If you die of what that leads you to do,
you are just like this woman on the floor.
She is an image of immoderation.

136

Remember her,
and keep your balance.

The maidservant returns and says, "Yes, you saw
my pleasure, but you didn't see the gourd
that put a limit on it. You opened
your shop before a Master
taught you the craft."

(*Mathnawi*, V, 1333-1405)

Chickpea to Cook

A chickpea leaps almost over the rim of the pot
where it's being boiled.

"Why are you doing this to me?"

The cook knocks him down with the ladle.

"Don't you try to jump out.
You think I'm torturing you.
I'm giving you flavor,
so you can mix with spices and rice
and be the lovely vitality of a human being.

Remember when you drank rain in the garden.
That was for this."

Grace first. Sexual pleasure,
then a boiling new life begins,
and the Friend has something good to eat.

Eventually the chickpea
will say to the cook,
                    "Boil me some more.
Hit me with the skimming spoon.
I can't do this by myself.

I'm like an elephant that dreams of gardens
back in Hindustan and doesn't pay attention
to his driver. You're my Cook, my Driver,

my Way into Existence. I love your cooking."

The Cook says,
          "I was once like you,
fresh from the ground. Then I boiled in Time,
and boiled in the Body, two fierce boilings.

My animal-soul grew powerful.
I controlled it with practices,
and boiled some more, and boiled
once beyond that,
                    and became your Teacher."

(*Mathnawi,* III, 4160-4168, 4197-4208)

139

A Presence Like Rain

There is a kind of spirit that comes
like fresh rain, a water
that carries away to the Ocean
whatever's foul and rotten.

There, water itself gets washed,
and the next year it comes again.

"Where have you been?"
                              "In the sea.
But now I'm ready again to accept all your filth.
Give it to me. Pull off your clothes,
and let me take them."

This is the magnificent work
of those watery souls
who wash us.

How could they shine,
if we were not so impure!

We exhaust their clarity with our silt,
and then the clouds lift them,
and the sun takes them as vapor.

In various molecular ways they go back
to the Ocean. What is meant by this Water
is the Spirit of the Enlightened Ones.

Think of these rivers and streams
as medicine shops. Let them take you
to be healed in that wide Water

where even they are cleaned.

Where, look, you can see
their cloudy robes
raining down.

(*Mathnawi*, V, 199-223)

NOTES

p. 30—Bayazid Bestami (d. 877) wrote nothing, but
many of his ecstatic sayings have been preserved:

"How great is my glory!"

"I am the wine-drinker and the wine and the cup-bearer."

"I came forth from Bayazid-ness as a snake from its skin.
Then I looked and saw that lover and Beloved are One."

"I was the smith of my own self."

"I am the Throne and the footstool."

"Your obedience to me is greater than my obedience to
You."

"I am the Well-preserved Tablet."

"I saw the Kaaba walking around me!"

Bestami illustrates the state of *fana,* of being so dissolved
in God that what is said is said by the Divine Presence. In
meditation Bestami developed an extremely daring sense
of the Numinous. His mystical experiences transcended
any distinctions between subject and object, and/or any
qualitites attributed to either. His utterances have been
preserved, and treasured, in Sufi circles for a thousand
years.

Bestami's teacher in this way of Mystical Union was Abu
Ali al-Sindi, who knew no Arabic. Bestami had to teach

his teacher enough Arabic to say the prayers from the *Qur'an*. In return, al-Sindi led Bestami deep into the path of meditation. Perhaps it could be said that in Bestami we find the blending of Islamic and Indian mysticisms into an unnameable, and wholly original, stream.

p. 37—Husam Chelebi was the scribe to whom Rumi dictated the entire *Mathnawi,* but he was also much more than this. Rumi said that Husam was the Source of the words. Rumi claimed only to be the flute. Husam was the fluteplayer and the breath, the *Mathnawi* itself being the song.

Husam was a student of Shams. It is through him, then, that the voice of the Beloved is made audible. Rumi says that Husam belongs to that class of saints who are not content with silent contemplation, but who must *express* their knowing.

p. 37—Daquqi's vision of the seven candles becoming one may refer to the Oneness of the Prophets, the essential Core of all religions, or it may refer to the Unity of the seven principle Divine Names (Living–*Hayy,* Knowing–*Alim,* Willing–*Murid,* Mighty–*Qadir,* Hearing–*Sami,* Seeing–*Basir,* and Speaking–*Mutakallim*), or it may refer to other mysteries.

p. 86—The Sun. Shams means "the Sun," and almost every use of that image in Rumi's poetry is meant as a remembrance of Shams of Tabriz, the wandering mystic whom Rumi met in 1244, when he was thirty-seven. Shams was perhaps fifty. Their Friendship is one of the central facts of mysticism. They merged in a duet of being that became a single note. Teacher and student, lover and Beloved, existence and Non-existence, light and the Source of Light, Presence and absence, all distinctions dissolved in the mystical conversation (*sohbet*) that they became. Rumi's entire collection of odes is called *The Works of Shams of Tabriz,* and Rumi referred to the *Mathnawi* as "The Book of Husam." Husam Chelebi, Rumi's scribe and a student of Shams, is always, as here, closely associated with Sunlight.

Annemarie Schimmel has a scholarly account of what is known about Shams in her *The Triumphal Sum: A Study of the Works of Jalaloddin Rumi,* East-West Publications (London, 1978), pp. 16–25. Aflaki, a 14th Century writer, gives the more legendary version. Excerpts from Aflaki can be found in a little booklet, *The Whirling Ecstasy,* distributed by Sufi Islamia, 65 Norwich St. San Francisco, CA 94110.

p. 122—Ismail al-Maghribi died around 900 A.D. and is said to be buried beside his teacher Alf ibn Razin under a carob tree on Mt. Sinai. This poem illustrates what Ansari says of him, "He had never known darkness. Where it was dark to other people, to him it was light."

Rumi's "Sheikh Maghribi" should be distinguished from Ahmad Khattu Maghribi (1336–1446), the 14th Century Indian Sufi poet.

145

Other Rumi Books and Tapes
may be ordered from:

Maypop Books,
196 Westview Drive
Athens, GA 30606
(404) 543-2148

Open Secret $8.00 1984. Odes, quatrains, resettings of the *Mathnawi*. Winner of Pushcart Writer's Choice Award.

Unseen Rain $8.00 1986. Quatrains.

We Are Three $7.50 1987. Odes, quatrains, and sections from the *Mathnawi*.

This Longing $9.00 1988. Sections of the *Mathnawi* and some of Rumi's Letters.

These Branching Moments $6.95 1988. 40 Odes.

Like This $7.50 1990. Additional Odes.

Delicious Laughter $7.50 1990. Rambunctious Teaching Stories from the *Mathnawi*.

Open Secret (audio cassette) $9.95. Coleman Barks and Dorothy Fadiman read Rumi poems to flute and violin accompaniments.

Poems of Rumi (a two-cassette package) $15.95. Robert Bly and Coleman Barks read Rumi's poems with various musical accompaniments: drum, flute, sitar, tablas, etc.

Please Add $1.00 postage and handling for the first item and 25¢ for each additional item.